T0365906

GENERALIZED FERMAT EQUATION

GENERALIZED FERMAT EQUATION

RAN VAN VO

authorHOUSE®

AuthorHouse™
1663 Liberty Drive
Bloomington, IN 47403
www.authorhouse.com
Phone: 1 (800) 839-8640

© *2015 Ran Van Vo. All rights reserved.*

No part of this book may be reproduced, stored in a retrieval system, or transmitted by any means without the written permission of the author.

Published by AuthorHouse 09/10/2015

ISBN: 978-1-5049-4724-4 (sc)
ISBN: 978-1-5049-4725-1 (e)

Library of Congress Control Number: 2015914707

Print information available on the last page.

Any people depicted in stock imagery provided by Thinkstock are models, and such images are being used for illustrative purposes only. Certain stock imagery © Thinkstock.

This book is printed on acid-free paper.

Because of the dynamic nature of the Internet, any web addresses or links contained in this book may have changed since publication and may no longer be valid. The views expressed in this work are solely those of the author and do not necessarily reflect the views of the publisher, and the publisher hereby disclaims any responsibility for them.

CONTENTS

INTRODUCTION

Recently, Mathematicians are interested in an algebraic equation with solution in which the coefficients (a, b, c), …the variables are integers, and the exponent approaches infinity, this is called the Diophantine equation, which is very difficult

Ex:

Diophantine equatins take the form:

$$ax + by = c$$
$$ax^n + by^n = cz^n$$
$$av^n + bx^n + cy^n = dz^n$$

Or

$$x_1^n + x_2^n + \dots x_k^n = z^n$$

…

Diophantine equations are named for the ancient Greek/ Alexandrian mathematician Diophantus

"Diophantus of Alexandria *(Ancient Greek:* Διόφαντος ὁ Ἀλεξανδρεύς; *born sometime between AD 201 and 215;*

died aged 84 sometime between AD 285 and 299), sometimes called "the father of algebra", was an Alexandrian Greek mathematician and the author of a series of books called Arithmetica, many of which are now lost. These texts deal with solving algebraic equations"

In mathematics, Diophantine equations are polynomial equations where the coefficients (a, b, c, …) and the unknowns (x, y, z, …) are the whole numbers, and exponent "n" approaches infinity.

Generalized Fermat Equation

The equation we'll examine is

$$x^n + y^n = c \cdot z^n$$

Where c is a positive integer. We wish to learn what conditions on n and c force the existence of a non-trivial solution (x, y, z), that is, $x \cdot y \cdot z \neq 0$. In other words, when is the equation $x^n + y^n = c \cdot z^n$ solvable (in nonzero integers)? The case $n = 1$ is easy: taking $x = y = c$ and $z = 2$, we conclude that non-trivial solutions always exist. The case $n = 2$ is somewhat more difficult. Let c' denote the square-free part of c, that is, the divisor of c which is the outcome after all factors of the form d^2 have been eliminated. The equation

$$x^2 + y^2 = c \cdot z^2$$

2

is solvable if and only if all odd prime factors of c' are equal to 1 modulo 4. (See Hardy and Wright's [1] discussion of Waring's problem for a proof.) Here are the first several values of c for which this condition holds:..."

Fermat Equation

$$x^n + y^n = c \cdot z^n$$

Fermat equation "$x^n + y^n = c \cdot z^n$" is only a special case of Diophantine Equation, so we can call it the *"Fermat equation"* or *"Diophantine equation"*.

The Fermat equation is a big challenge for us. Diophantine Equation has over 2000 years, and are still difficult problems.

In the XX century, mathematicians were very interested in the great problems, also Professor Andrew Wiles was very concerned about this equation "$x^n + y^n = c \cdot z^n$", thus the mathematicians named as: *"Fermat-Wiles Equation"*

Then *"Fermat-Wiles Equation"* is very difficult problems

"Mathematicians have always been fascinated by the problem of describing all solutions in whole numbers x,y,z to algebraic equations like

$$x^2 + y^2 = z^2$$

3

Euclid gave the complete solution for that equation, but for more complicated equations this becomes extremely difficult. Indeed, in 1970 Yu. V. Matiyasevich showed that Hilbert's tenth problem is unsolvable, i.e., **there is no general method for determining when such equations have a solution in whole numbers...***"*

GENERAL METHOD

We find the general method for solution of the equation

$$x^n + y^n = c \cdot z^n \text{ with exponent } n = 2$$

*) Find the value of c of the equation below for the values of x, y, z are the whole numbers

$$x^2 + y^2 = c \cdot z^2$$

Solve

First we must find the value of c
On internet we see

http://www.mathsoft.com/mathsoft_resources/unsolved_problems/2186a.aspx
"1, 2, 5, 10, 13, 17, 26, 29, 34, 37, 41, 53, 58, 61, 65, 73, 74, 82, 85, 89, 97, 101, 106, 109, 113, 122, 130, 137, 145, 146, 149, 157, 170, 173, 178, 181, 185, 193, 194, 197, 202, 205, 218, 221, 226, 229, 233, 241, 257, 265, 269, 274, 277, 281, 290, 293, 298, 305, 313, 314, 317, 337, 346, 349, 353, 362, 365, 370, 373, 377,

386, 389, 394, 397, 401, 409, 410, 421, 433, 442, 445, 449, 457, 458, 461, 466, 481, 482, 485, 493, ..."

Mathematicians used the following method:

Landau-Ramanujan Constant
"It can be proved that

$$\lim_{N \to \infty} \delta(N) = 0$$

$$\lim_{N \to \infty} \sqrt{\ln(N) \cdot \delta(N)} = K$$

And, more precisely,

Where K = 0.764223653... is known as the Landau-Ramanujan constan.

Landau-Ramanujan Constant

Let B(x) denote the number of positive integers not exceeding x which can be expressed as a sum of two squares. E. Landau and S. Ramanujan independently proved that:

$$\lim_{x \to \infty} \frac{\ln(x)^{\frac{1}{2}}}{x} \cdot B(x) = K$$

Where K is given by:

$$K = \left[\frac{1}{2} \prod_{\substack{p \text{ prime} \\ p = 4 \cdot k + 3}} \frac{1}{1 - p^{-2}} \cdot B(x) \right]^{\frac{1}{2}} = 0.764223653$$

6

Product taken over all primes congruent to 3 modulo 4

Landau further proved that

$$\lim_{x \to \infty} \frac{\ln(x)^{\frac{3}{2}}}{K \cdot x} \cdot \left(B(x) - \frac{K \cdot x}{\sqrt{\ln(x)}} \right) = C$$

Where C is the constant

$$C = \frac{1}{2} \left(1 - \ln\left(\frac{\pi}{2 \cdot L} \cdot e^y \right) \right) - \frac{1}{4} \cdot \frac{d}{ds} \ln\left(\prod_{\substack{p \text{ prime} \\ p = 4k+3}} \frac{1}{1 - p^{-2s}} \right)\Bigg|_{s=1} ,$$

..."

GENERAL POPULAR METHOD

The method of *Landau-Ramanujan Constant* is very difficult, therefore I found another method below

We get the Diophantine equation

$$x^n + y^n = c \cdot z^n$$

Divided both sides of the Diophantine equation above by z^n ($z \neq 0$)

$$x^n/z^n + y^n/z^n = c$$
$$(x/z)^n + (y/z)^n = c$$

Put:
$$r = x/z \text{ and } s = y/z$$

We get:
$$r^n + s^n = c$$

(r and s are integers or rational numbers, and c is the whole number)

We find the value of c of the Diophantine equation "$x^n + y^n = c \cdot z^n$" also known as FERMAT-WILES EQUATION by new method

$$r^n + s^n = c$$

The values of x, y, z calculated by r & s as following

$$x = r \cdot z$$

$$y = s \cdot z$$

And my General Method:

$$\zeta(s) = r^n + s^n = c$$

$$s = \sqrt[n]{c - r^n}$$
$$r = \sqrt[n]{c - s^n}$$
$$\zeta(s) = c \ \& \ \zeta(c) = 0$$
$$x = r \cdot z = \sqrt[n]{c - s^n} \cdot z$$
$$y = s \cdot z = \sqrt[n]{c - r^n} \cdot z$$

$$n \rightarrow \infty$$

$\zeta(s)$: zeta function (i.e., r, s, t, u, …. Rational numbers or whole numbers)

c: coefficients of right side of Diophantine equation (i.e., c, d, e, … Whole numbers)

$\zeta(s) = c$ & $\zeta(c) = 0$ (Rational number)

…., x, y, z,: unknowns (whole numbers)

My General method can be called *the popular method*

We find the values of c by my popular method

$$\zeta(s) = r^n + s^n = c$$

$$s = \sqrt[n]{c - r^n}$$
$$r = \sqrt[n]{c - s^n}$$
$$\zeta(s) = c \ \& \ \zeta(c) = 0$$
$$x = r \cdot z = \sqrt[n]{c - s^n \cdot z}$$
$$y = s \cdot z = \sqrt[n]{c - r^n \cdot z}$$

$$n \to \infty$$

For example: n = 2

$$0.6^2 + 0.8^2 = 1$$
$$1^2 + 1^2 = 1.4^2 + 0.2^2 = 2$$
$$(48/25)^2 + (14/25)^2 = 4 = 1.6^2 + 1.2^2 = (24/13)^2 + (10/13)^2$$
$$1^2 + 2^2 = 2.2^2 + 0.4^2 = 5$$
$$2.8^2 + 0.4^2 = 2^2 + 2^2 = 8$$
$$(120/41)^2 + (27/41)^2 = 9 = 1.8^2 + 2.4^2 = (180/61)^2 + (33/61)^2$$
$$1^2 + 3^2 = 1.8^2 + 2.6^2 = 10$$
$$1.2^2 + 3.4^2 = 2^2 + 3^2 = 13 = 3.6^2 + 0.2^2$$
$$3.2^2 + 2.4^2 = 16$$
$$1^2 + 4^2 = 1.6^2 + 3.8^2 = 17$$
$$0.6^2 + 4.2^2 = 3^2 + 3^2 = 18$$
$$0.8^2 + 4.4^2 = 2^2 + 4^2 = 20$$
$$3^2 + 4^2 = 25$$
$$1^2 + 5^2 = 2.2^2 + 4.6^2 = 26 = 3.4^2 + 3.8^2$$

....

On internet we see (n = 2)

(See Hardy and Wright's[1] discussion of Waring's problem for a proof.) Here are the first several values of c for which this condition holds:

"1, 2, 4, 10, 13, 17, 26, 29, 34, 37, 41, 53, 58, 61, 65, 73, 74, 82, 85, 89, 97, 101, 106, 109, 113, 122, 130, 137, 145, 146, 149, 157, 170, 173, 178, 181, 185, 193, 194, 197, 202, 205, 218, 221, 226, 229, 233, 241, 257, 265, 269, 274, 277, 281, 290, 293, 298, 305, 313, 314, 317, 337, 346, 349, 353, 362, 365, 370, 373, 377, 386, 389, 394, 397, 401, 409, 410, 421, 433, 442, 445, 449, 457, 458, 461, 466, 481, 482, 485, 493 ..."

The value of c on internet

"1, 2, 5, 10, 13, 17, 26 ...."

Applying my popular method, I can find more the value of c:
$$4, 8, 9, 18, 20, 25 \ldots$$

Then my list
$$1, 2, 4, 5, 8, 9, 10, 13, 17, 18, 20, 25, 26\ldots$$

Example1:

c = 4, we have the Diophantine equation
$$x^2 + y^2 = 4 \cdot z^2$$

Applying my popular method

$$r^2 + s^2 = c$$

The value of c = 4

$$r^2 + s^2 = c = 4$$
$$1.2^2 + 1.6^2 = 4$$
$$(24/13)^2 + (10/13)^2 = 4$$

We have

$$r_1 = 1.2, s_1 = 1.6$$
$$r_2 = 24/13, s_2 = 10/13$$

Applying the popular method

$$\zeta(s) = r^n + s^n = c$$

$$s = \sqrt[n]{c - r^n}$$
$$r = \sqrt[n]{c - s^n}$$
$$\zeta(s) = c \ \& \ \zeta(c) = 0$$
$$x = r \cdot z = \sqrt[n]{c - s^n \cdot z}$$
$$y = s \cdot z = \sqrt[n]{c - r^n \cdot z}$$

$$n \to \infty$$

The values of x_1, y_1, z_1

$$x_1 = r_1 \cdot z_1$$
$$x_1 = 1.2 \cdot z_1$$

Choose $z_1 = 5$ or mod 5

$$x_1 = 1.2 \times 5 = 6$$

And value of y_1

$$y_1 = s_1 \cdot z_1$$
$$y_1 = 1.6 \times 5 = 8$$

Try again

Replace the values of x, y, z, into the Diophantine equation

$$x^2 + y^2 = 4 \cdot z^2$$
$$6^2 + 8^2 = 4 \cdot 5^2 = 100$$

Solution: x = 6, y = 8, z = 5

The values of x_2, y_2, z_2

$$r_2 = 24/13, \ s_2 = 10/13$$
$$x_2 = r_2 \cdot z_2$$
$$x_2 = (24/13) \cdot z_2$$

Choose $z_2 = 13$ or mod 13

$$x_2 = (24/13) \times 13 = 24$$

And the value of y_2

$$y_2 = s_2 \cdot z_2$$
$$y_2 = (10/13) \times 13 = 10$$

Try again

Replace the values of x, y, z, into the Diophantine equation

$$x^2 + y^2 = 4 \cdot z^2$$
$$24^2 + 10^2 = 4 \cdot 13^2 = 676$$

Solution: x = 24, y = 10, z = 13

Example 2:

c = 25, we have the Diophantine equation

$$x^2 + y^2 = 25 \cdot z^2$$

Applying my popular method

$$r^2 + s^2 = c$$

The value of c = 25

$$r^2 + s^2 = c = 25$$
$$3^2 + 4^2 = 25$$

We have

$$r = 3, \ s = 4$$

Applying the popular method

$$\zeta(s) = r^n + s^n = c$$

$$s = \sqrt[n]{c - r^n}$$
$$r = \sqrt[n]{c - s^n}$$
$$\zeta(s) = c \ \& \ \zeta(c) = 0$$
$$x = r \cdot z = \sqrt[n]{c - s^n} \cdot z$$
$$y = s \cdot z = \sqrt[n]{c - r^n} \cdot z$$

$$n \to \infty$$

The values of x, y, z

$$x = r \cdot z$$
$$x = 3 \cdot z$$

Choose any value of z (i.e., 1, 2, 3, 4, 5, 6, …)

$$x = 3 \times 6 = 18$$

And value of y

$$y = s \cdot z$$
$$x = 4 \times 6 = 24$$

Try again

Replace the values of x, y, z, into the Diophantine equation

$$x^2 + y^2 = 25 \cdot z^2$$
$$18^2 + 24^2 = 25 \cdot 6^2 = 900$$

Solution: x = 18, y = 24, z = 6

Other solution:

$$x = 51, y = 68, z = 17$$

Replace the values of x, y, z, into the Diophantine equation for try again

$$x2 + y2 = 25 \cdot z2$$
$$512 + 682 = 25 \cdot 172$$
$$2601 + 4624 = 7225$$

The method of *Landau-Ramanujan Constant* is very difficult, but it's not yet the method for finding the values of x, y, z

$$\lim_{x \to \infty} \frac{\ln(x)^{\frac{1}{2}}}{x} \cdot B(x) = K$$

Where K is given by:

$$K = \left[\frac{1}{2} \prod_{\substack{p \text{ prime} \\ p = 4 \cdot k + 3}} \frac{1}{1 - p^{-2}} \cdot B(x) \right]^{\frac{1}{2}} = 0.764223653$$

15

Product taken over all primes congruent to 3 modulo 4

Landau further proved that

$$\lim_{x \to \infty} \frac{\ln(x)^{\frac{3}{2}}}{K \cdot x} \cdot \left(B(x) - \frac{K \cdot x}{\sqrt{\ln(x)}} \right) = C$$

Where C is the constant

$$C = \frac{1}{2} \left(1 - \ln\left(\frac{\pi}{2 \cdot L} \cdot e^y \right) \right) - \frac{1}{4} \cdot \frac{d}{ds} \ln\left(\prod_{\substack{p \text{ prime} \\ p=4 \cdot k+3}} \frac{1}{1-p^{-2s}} \right)\Bigg|_{s=1} \quad ..."$$

On internet we see

The method for finding the value of x, y, z, of Professor Selmer following with n = 3

"Selmer[2] additionally listed sample solutions (x, y, z) for each of the above c-values; we give just a few here:

C	X	Y	Z
2	1	1	1
6	37	17	21
7	2	-1	1
9	2	1	1
12	89	19	39
13	7	2	3
15	683	397	294
17	18	-1	7
19	3	-2	1
20	19	1	7
22	25469	17299	9954
26	3	-1	1
28	3	1	1

APPLICATION

An example of my popular method for finding the solution of the Diophantine equation, or "Fermat-Wiles Equations" is demonstrated below.

*) Find the value for all unknowns of the Diophantine equation

$$\frac{x^2 + y^2}{z^2} = k,$$ all the unknowns must take the whole numbers

Given k = 13

Solve

Diophantine equation

$$\frac{x^2 + y^2}{z^2} = k,$$

3 unknowns (x, y, z)

$$(x^2 + y^2)/z^2 = k$$

I write back to form Fermat-Wiles Equation

$$x^2 + y^2 = k \cdot z^2$$

k is equivalent to c of Fermat-Wiles Equation

$$x^2 + y^2 = c \cdot z^2$$

Applying the popular method

$$r^2 + s^2 = c$$

We have the value of k or c equal to 13

$$r^2 + s^2 = c = 13$$
$$1.2^2 + 3.4^2 = 13$$
$$0.2^2 + 3.6^2 = 13$$
$$2^2 + 3^2 = 13$$

We have

$$r_1 = 1.2, s_1 = 3.4$$
$$r_2 = 0.2, s_2 = 3.6$$
$$r_3 = 2, s_3 = 3$$

Applying the popular method

$$\zeta(s) = r^n + s^n = c$$

$$s = \sqrt[n]{c - r^n}$$
$$r = \sqrt[n]{c - s^n}$$
$$\zeta(s) = c \ \& \ \zeta(c) = 0$$
$$x = r \cdot z = \sqrt[n]{c - s^n} \cdot z$$
$$y = s \cdot z = \sqrt[n]{c - r^n} \cdot z$$

$$n \to \infty$$

The values of x_1, y_1, z_1

$$x_1 = r_1 \cdot z_1$$
$$x_1 = 1.2 \cdot z_1$$

Choose $z_1 = 5$

$$x_1 = 1.2 \times 5 = 6$$

And value of y_1

$$y_1 = s_1 \cdot z_1$$
$$y_1 = 3.4 \times 5 = 17$$

Try again

Replace the values of x, y, z, into the Diophantine equation

$$x^2 + y^2 = 13 \cdot z^2$$
$$6^2 + 17^2 = 13 \cdot 5^2 = 325$$

Or

$$(x^2 + y^2)/z^2 = 13$$
$$(6^2 + 17^2)/5^2 = 13$$

The values of x_2, y_2, z_2

$$x_2 = r_2 \cdot z_2$$
$$x_2 = 0.2 \cdot z_2$$

Choose $z_2 = 5$

$$x_2 = 0.2 \times 5 = 1$$

And the value of y_2

$$y_2 = s_2 \cdot z_2$$
$$y_2 = 3.6 \times 5 = 18$$

Try again

Replace the values of x, y, z, into the Diophantine equation

$$x^2 + y^2 = 13 \cdot z^2$$
$$1^2 + 18^2 = 13 \cdot 5^2 = 325$$

Or

$$(x^2 + y^2)/z^2 = 13$$
$$(1^2 + 18^2)/5^2 = 13$$

The values of x_3, y_3, z_3

$$x_3 = r_3 \cdot z_3$$
$$x_3 = 2 \cdot z_3$$

Choose $z_3 = 1$ smallest value for x_3 is an integer

$$x_3 = 2 \times 1 = 2$$
$$y_3 = s_3 \cdot z_3$$
$$y_3 = 3 \times 1 = 3$$

Try again

Replace the values of x, y, z, into the Diophantine equation

$$(x^2 + y^2)/z^2 = 13$$
$$(2^2 + 3^2)/1^2 = 13$$

Solution 1)

$$x_1 = 6, y_1 = 17, z_1 = 5$$

Solution 2)

$$x_2 = 1, y_2 = 18, z_2 = 5$$

Solution 3)

$$x_3 = 2, y_3 = 3, z_3 = 1$$

*) Find the values of x, y, z of the Diophantine equation

$$\frac{x^2 + y^2}{z^2} = k, \text{ all the unknowns take integer values}$$

Given k = 17

Solve

Diophantine equation

$$\frac{x^2 + y^2}{z^2} = k,$$

Write back to form Fermat-Wiles Equation

$$x^2 + y^2 = k \cdot z^2$$

k is equivalent to c of Fermat-Wiles Equation

$$x^2 + y^2 = c \cdot z^2$$

Applying the popular method

$$r^2 + s^2 = c$$

We have the value of k or c equal to 17

$$r^2 + s^2 = c = 17$$
$$1^2 + 4^2 = 1.6^2 + 3.8^2 = 17$$

Then

$$1^2 + 4^2 = 17$$
$$1.6^2 + 3.8^2 = 17$$

We have

$$r_1 = 1, s_1 = 4$$
$$r_2 = 1.6, s_1 = 3.8$$

We apply the popular method

$$\zeta(s) = r^n + s^n = c$$

$$s = \sqrt[n]{c - r^n}$$
$$r = \sqrt[n]{c - s^n}$$
$$\zeta(s) = c \;\&\; \zeta(c) = 0$$
$$x = r \cdot z = \sqrt[n]{c - s^n \cdot z}$$
$$y = s \cdot z = \sqrt[n]{c - r^n \cdot z}$$

$$n \to \infty$$

The values of x_1, y_1, z_1

$$x_1 = r_1 \cdot z_1$$
$$x_1 = 1 \cdot z_1$$

We choose any value of z_1 (i.e., 1, 2, 3, 4, …)

$$x_1 = 1 \times 4 = 4$$

And value of y_1

$$y_1 = s_1 \cdot z_1$$
$$y_1 = 4 \times 4 = 16$$

Try again

$$(x^2 + y^2)/z^2 = 17$$
$$(4^2 + 16^2)/4^2 = 17$$

The values of x_2, y_2, z_2

$$x_2 = r_2 \cdot z_2$$
$$x_2 = 1.6 \cdot z_2$$

Choose $z_2 = 5$

$$x_2 = 1.6 \times 5 = 8$$

And the value of y_2

$$y_2 = s_2 \cdot z_2$$
$$y_2 = 3.8 \times 5 = 19$$

Try again

$$(x^2 + y^2)/z^2 = 17$$
$$(8^2 + 19^2)/5^2 = 17$$

Solution 1)

$$x_1 = 4, y_1 = 16, z_1 = 4$$

Solution 2)

$$x_2 = 8, y_2 = 19, z_2 = 5$$

---

*) Find the values of x, y, z of the Diophantine equation

$$\frac{x^2 + y^2}{z^2} = k, = k,$$ all the unknowns take integer values

Given k = 20

23

Solve

Diophantine equation

$$\frac{x^2 + y^2}{z^2} = k,$$

Write back to form Fermat-Wiles Equation

$$x^2 + y^2 = k \cdot z^2$$

k is equivalent to c of Fermat-Wiles Equation

$$x^2 + y^2 = c \cdot z^2$$

Applying the popular method

$$r^2 + s^2 = c$$

We have the value of k or c equal to 20

$$r^2 + s^2 = c = 20$$
$$0.8^{\wedge}2 + 4.4^{\wedge}2 = 2^{\wedge}2 + 4^{\wedge}2 = 20$$
$$0.8^2 + 4.4^2 = 20$$
$$2^2 + 4^2 = 20$$

We have

$$r_1 = 0.8, \, s_1 = 4.4$$
$$r_2 = 2, \, s_2 = 4$$

We apply the popular method

$$\zeta(s) = r^n + s^n = c$$

$$s = \sqrt[n]{c - r^n}$$
$$r = \sqrt[n]{c - s^n}$$
$$\zeta(s) = c \ \& \ \zeta(c) = 0$$
$$x = r \cdot z = \sqrt[n]{c - s^n} \cdot z$$
$$y = s \cdot z = \sqrt[n]{c - r^n} \cdot z$$

$$n \to \infty$$

a) The values of x_1, y_1, z_1

$$x_1 = r_1 \cdot z_1$$
$$x_1 = 0.8 \cdot z_1$$

Choose $z_1 = 10$ for x_1 is whole number

$$x_1 = 0.8 \times 10 = 8$$

And value of y_1

$$y_1 = s_1 \cdot z_1$$
$$y_1 = 4.4 \times 10 = 44$$

Try again

$$(x^2 + y^2)/z^2 = 20$$
$$(8^2 + 44^2)/10^2 = 20$$

b) The values of x_2, y_2, z_2

$$x_2 = r_2 \cdot z_2$$
$$x_2 = 2 \cdot z_2$$

25

Choose $z_2 = 3$

$$x_2 = 2 \times 3 = 6$$

And the value of y_2

$$y_2 = s_2 \cdot z_2$$
$$y_2 = 4 \times 3 = 12$$

Try again

$$(x^2 + y^2)/z^2 = 20$$
$$(6^2 + 12^2)/3^2 = 20$$

Solution 1)

$$x_1 = 8, y_1 = 44, z_1 = 10$$

Solution 2)

$$x_2 = 6, y_2 = 12, z_2 = 3$$

―――――――――――――

SUMMARY

Here, I am applying my popular method for the Diophantine equation or Fermat-Wiles Equation below:

$$\text{``}x^n + y^n = c \cdot z^n\text{''} \ (n \longrightarrow \infty),$$

$$\zeta(s) = r^n + s^n = c$$

$$s = \sqrt[n]{c - r^n}$$
$$r = \sqrt[n]{c - s^n}$$
$$\zeta(s) = c \ \& \ \zeta(c) = 0$$
$$x = r \cdot z = \sqrt[n]{c - s^n} \cdot z$$
$$y = s \cdot z = \sqrt[n]{c - r^n} \cdot z$$

$$n \to \infty$$

EXERCISES

*) Find the values of x, y, z of the Diophantine equation
$\dfrac{x^2 + y^2}{z^2} = k,$ all the unknowns take integer values

Given k = 130

*) Find the values of x, y, z of the Diophantine equation
$\dfrac{x^2 + y^2}{z^2} = k,$ all the unknowns take integer values

Given k = 100

*) Find the values of x, y, z of the Diophantine equation
$\dfrac{x^2 + y^2}{z^2} = k,$ all the unknowns take integer values

Given k = 65

*) Find the values of x, y, z of the Diophantine equation $\dfrac{x^2 + y^2}{z^2} = k$, all the unknowns take integer values

Given k = 250

*) Find the values of x, y, z of the Diophantine equation $\dfrac{x^2 + y^2}{z^2} = k$, all the unknowns take integer values

Given k = 80

*) Find the values of x, y, z of the Diophantine equation $\dfrac{x^2 + y^2}{z^2} = k$, all the unknowns take integer values

Given k = 370

*) Find the values of x, y, z of the Diophantine equation $\dfrac{x^2 + y^2}{z^2} = k$, all the unknowns take integer values

Given k = 233

*) Find the values of x, y, z of the Diophantine equation $\frac{x^2+y^2}{z^2}=k,$ all the unknowns take integer values

Given k = 225

*) Find the values of x, y, z of the Diophantine equation $\frac{x^2+y^2}{z^2}=k,$ all the unknowns take integer values

Given k = 229

DIOPHANTINE EQUATION (N = 2)

$$a{\cdot}x^n + b{\cdot}y^n = c{\cdot}z^n$$

The Diophantine equation of oldest Babylonian (1800-1600 BCE)

$$2x^2 - y^2 = 1$$

Applying my popular method for the Diophantine Equations of oldest Babylonian

$$2x^2 - y^2 = 1$$

Solve

Rewrite equation

$$2x^2 - y^2 = 1$$

To Fermat-Wiles equation

$$x^n + y^n = c{\cdot}x^n$$

Or

$$1^2 + y^2 = 2x^2$$

Applying popular method

$$\zeta(s) = r^n + s^n = c$$

$$s = \sqrt[n]{c - r^n}$$
$$r = \sqrt[n]{c - s^n}$$
$$\zeta(s) = c \ \& \ \zeta(c) = 0$$
$$x = r \cdot z = \sqrt[n]{c - s^n \cdot z}$$
$$y = s \cdot z = \sqrt[n]{c - r^n \cdot z}$$

$$n \to \infty$$

Back to equation

$$1^2 + y^2 = 2x^2 \ (z \ \text{replace} \ x)$$

Equations of ancient Babylon

$$c = 2 \ \text{and} \ z = 1$$

Find the value of r and s

$$r^2 + s^2 = 2$$
$$1^2 + 1^2 = 2$$
$$0.2^2 + 1.4^2 = 2$$

We have

$$r_1 = 1, s_1 = 1$$
$$r_2 = 0.2, s_2 = 1.4$$

Replace the value of r & s to find the value of x, y

$$1 = r_1 \cdot x_1 \ (\text{replace} \ z = x_1) \to x_1 = 1/r_1 = 1/1 = 1$$
$$y_1 = s_1 \cdot x_1 = 1 \cdot 1 = 1$$

Try again

$$2x^2 - y^2 = 1$$
$$2 \cdot 1^2 - 1^2 = 1$$
$$2 - 1 = 1$$

And other values of $r_2 = 0.2$, $s_2 = 1.4$

$$1 = r_2 \cdot x_2 \longrightarrow x_2 = 1/r_2 = 1/0.2 = 5$$
$$y_2 = s_2 \cdot x_2 \longrightarrow y = 5 \times 1.4 = 7$$

Try again

$$2x^2 - y^2 = 1$$
$$2 \cdot 5^2 - 7^2 = 1$$
$$50 - 49 = 1$$

Solution 1

$$x_1 = 1 \text{ and } y_1 = 1$$

Solution 2

$$x_2 = 5 \text{ and } y_2 = 7$$

…

————————————————

*) Find the values of x and y of the Diophantine equation
$$13x^2 - y^2 = 1$$

The solutions sought are also integers.

Solve

Similarly we rewrite the above equation as
$$1 + y^2 = 13x^2$$

This equation $1^2 + y^2 = 13x^2$
Fermat Wiles Equation
$$x^n + y^n = c{\cdot}x^n$$

Applying my method
$$\zeta(s) = r^n + s^n = c$$

Find the values of r, s
$$r^2 + s^2 = 13$$
$$3.6^2 + 0.2^2 = 41$$

We have
$$r = 0.2,\ s = 3.6$$

Applying the popular method

$$x{=}r \cdot z{=}^n\sqrt{c - s^n \cdot z}$$
$$y{=}s \cdot z{=}^n\sqrt{c - r^n \cdot z}$$

$$n \to \infty$$

Find the values of x, y
Replace the value of r & s to find the value of x, y
$x = r \cdot z$ (replace z = x) $\to$ x = 1/r = 1/0.2 = 5
$y = s \cdot z$ (replace z = x) = 3.6 · 5 = 18

Try again

$$13 \cdot x^2 - y^2 = 1$$
$$13 \cdot 5^2 - 18^2 = 1$$
$$325 - 324 = 1$$

Solution

$$x = 5 \text{ and } y = 18$$

*) Find the values of x and y of the Diophantine equation
$$26x^2 - y^2 = 1$$

The solutions sought are also integers.

Solve

Similarly we rewrite the equation
$$26x^2 - y^2 = 1$$

To Fermat - Wiles equation
$$1 + y^2 = 26x^2$$

This equation $1^2 + y^2 = 26x^2$ has form Fermat -Wiles Equation
$$x^n + y^n = c \cdot x^n$$

Applying my popular method
$$\zeta(s) = r^n + s^n = c$$

Find the values of r, s

$$r^2 + s^2 = 26$$
$$1^2 + 5^2 = 26$$
$$2.2^2 + 4.6^2 = 26$$
$$3.4^2 + 3.8^2 = 26$$

We have

$$r_1 = 1, s_1 = 5$$
$$r_2 = 2.2, s_1 = 4.6$$
$$r_2 = 3.4, s_3 = 3.8$$

Applying the popular method

$$\zeta(s) = r^n + s^n = c$$

$$s = \sqrt[n]{c - r^n}$$
$$r = \sqrt[n]{c - s^n}$$
$$\zeta(s) = c \,\&\, \zeta(c) = 0$$
$$x = r \cdot z = \sqrt[n]{c - s^n} \cdot z$$
$$y = s \cdot z = \sqrt[n]{c - r^n} \cdot z$$

$$n \rightarrow \infty$$

The values of x_1, y_1, z_1

Replace the value of r & s to find the the value of x, y

$$1 = r_1 \cdot x_1 \,(\text{replace } z = x_1) \longrightarrow x_1 = 1/r_1 = 1/1 = 1$$
$$y_1 = s_1 \cdot x_1 = 5 \cdot 1 = 5$$

Replace the values of x, y into the equation for try again

$$26x^2 - y^2 = 1$$
$$26 \cdot 1^2 - 5^2 = 1$$
$$26 - 25 = 1$$

Other values of $r_2 = 2.2$, $s_2 = 4.6$

$1 = r_2 \cdot x_2 \rightarrow x_2 = 1/r_2 = 1/2.2 = 0.4545454545\ldots$

$y_2 = s_2 \cdot x_2 \rightarrow y_2 = 4.6 \times 0.45454545\ldots = 2.09090909\ldots$

The values of x_2, y_2 are not the whole numbers

Similarly

And other values of $r_3 = 3.4$, $s_3 = 3.8$

The values of x_3, y_3 are not the whole numbers

Then solution of the equation

$$26x^2 - y^2 = 1$$
$$x = 1 \text{ and } y = 5$$

---

*) Find the values of x and y of the Diophantine equation

$$41x^2 - y^2 = 1$$

The solutions sought are also integers.

Solve

Similarly we rewrite the above equation as

$$1 + y^2 = 41x^2$$

This equation $1^2 + y^2 = 41x^2$

Fermat Wiles Equation

$$x^n + y^n = c \cdot x^n$$

37

Applying my method

$$\zeta(s) = r^n + s^n = c$$

Find the values of r, s

$$r^2 + s^2 = 41$$
$$6.4^2 + 0.2^2 = 41$$

We have

$$r = 0.2, \ s = 6.4$$

Applying the popular method

$$x = r \cdot z = \sqrt[n]{c - s^n \cdot z}$$
$$y = s \cdot z = \sqrt[n]{c - r^n \cdot z}$$
$$n \to \infty$$

Find the values of x, y

Replace the value of r & s to find the value of x, y

$x = r \cdot z$ (replace $z = x$) $\longrightarrow x = 1/r = 1/0.2 = 5$
$y = s \cdot z$ (replace $z = x$) $= 6.4 \cdot 5 = 32$

Try again

$$41 \cdot x^2 - y^2 = 1$$
$$41 \cdot 5^2 - 32^2 = 1$$
$$1025 - 1024 = 1$$

Solution

$$x = 5 \text{ and } y = 32$$

_____

EXERCISES

*) Find the values of x and y of the Diophantine equation

$$17x^2 - y^2 = 1$$

The solutions sought are also integers.

*) Find the values of x and y of the Diophantine equation

$$37x^2 - y^2 = 1$$

The solutions sought are also integers.

*) Find the values of x and y of the Diophantine equation

$$50x^2 - y^2 = 1$$

The solutions sought are also integers.

*) Find the values of x and y of the Diophantine equation

$$65x^2 - y^2 = 1$$

The solutions sought are also integers.

*) Find the values of x and y of the Diophantine equation

$$74x^2 - y^2 = 1$$

The solutions sought are also integers.

*) Find the values of x and y of the Diophantine equation

$$101x^2 - y^2 = 1$$

The solutions sought are also integers.

*) Find the values of x and y of the Diophantine equation

$$122x^2 - y^2 = 1$$

The solutions sought are also integers.

*) Find the values of x and y of the Diophantine equation

$$130x^2 - y^2 = 1$$

The solutions sought are also integers.

*) Find the values of x and y of the Diophantine equation

$$170x^2 - y^2 = 1$$

The solutions sought are also integers.

*) Find the values of x and y of the Diophantine equation

$$185x^2 - y^2 = 1$$

The solutions sought are also integers.

*) Find the values of x and y of the Diophantine equation

$$197x^2 - y^2 = 1$$

The solutions sought are also integers.

*) Find the values of x and y of the Diophantine equation

$$269x^2 - y^2 = 1$$

The solutions sought are also integers.

*) Find the values of x and y of the Diophantine equation

$$346x^2 - y^2 = 1$$

The solutions sought are also integers.

APPLICATION

*) There are 100 balls in 3 different colors of blue, yellow, and purple.

Given square blue, and yellow balls, the sum of both, is equal to the multiple of 5 by square purple balls

How many balls of each color?

Solve

We put

A= blue balls,

B = yellow balls,

C = purple balls

Hypothesis that

$$F_1(s) = A + B + C = 100$$

And

$$F_2(s) = A^2 + B^2 = 5.C^2$$

Applying the popular method

$$\zeta(s) = r^n + s^n = c$$

$$s = \sqrt[n]{c - r^n}$$
$$r = \sqrt[n]{c - s^n}$$
$$\zeta(s) = c \ \& \ \zeta(c) = 0$$
$$x = r \cdot z = \sqrt[n]{c - s^n \cdot z}$$
$$y = s \cdot z = \sqrt[n]{c - r^n \cdot z}$$

$$n \to \infty$$

The values of A, C, B

$$\zeta(s) = c \text{ and } \zeta(c) = 0$$
$$\zeta(s) = r^2 + s^2 = 5$$
$$A = r \cdot C$$
$$B = s \cdot C$$

Find the value of r and s

We have

$$\zeta(s) = 1^2 + 2^2 = 2.2^2 + 0.4^2 = 5$$

The first approach to

$$\zeta(s) = 1^2 + 2^2 = 5$$
$$A = 1 \cdot C$$
$$B = 2 \cdot C$$
$$C = 100/4 = 25 \text{ balls}$$

$$A = 1C = 1 \cdot 25 = 25 \text{ balls}$$
$$B = 2C = 2 \cdot 25 = 50 \text{ balls}$$

Try again

Replace these values into $F_1(s)$ and $F_2(s)$

$$F_1(s) = A + B + C = 100$$
$$= 25 + 50 + 25 = 100$$

And

$$F_2(s) = A^2 + B^2 = 5 \cdot C^2$$
$$F_2(s) = 25^2 + 50^2 \equiv 5 \cdot 25^2 = 3125$$

Soluion 1:

A: 25 balls

B: 50 -

C: 25 -

The second approach to

$$\zeta(s) = 2.2^2 + 0.4^2 = 5$$

We just received the answer of integers

$$A = 2.2 \cdot C$$
$$B = 0.4 \cdot C$$
$$C = 100/3.6 = 27.777777777778 \text{ (we do not get)}$$

Solution:

A = blue balls: 25

B = yellow balls: 50

C = purple balls: 25

*) The balls are three different colors, green, yellow and purple

We square blue, and yellow balls, then sum of both, it's equal to multiple of 13 with square purple balls

How many balls of each color

Given: 45 purple balls

Solve

We put

A= green balls

B = yellow balls

C = purple balls

We have

$$F_1(s) = A^2 + B^2 = 13.C^2$$

Applying the popular method n = 2

$$\zeta(s) = r^n + s^n = c$$

$$s = \sqrt[n]{c - r^n}$$
$$r = \sqrt[n]{c - s^n}$$
$$\zeta(s) = c \ \& \ \zeta(c) = 0$$
$$x = r \cdot z = \sqrt[n]{c - s^n \cdot z}$$
$$y = s \cdot z = \sqrt[n]{c - r^n \cdot z}$$

$$n \to \infty$$

The values of A, B, C

$$\zeta(s) = c \text{ and } \zeta(c) = 0$$
$$\zeta(s) = r^2 + s^2 = 13$$
$$A = r \cdot C$$
$$B = s \cdot C$$

Find the values of r and s

$$\zeta(s) = 2^2 + 3^2 = 13$$
$$1.2^2 + 3.4^2 = 13$$
$$0.2^2 + 3.6^2 = 13$$

The first approach to

$$\zeta(s) = 2^2 + 3^2 = 13$$
$$A = 2 \cdot C$$
$$B = 3 \cdot C$$

The values of A, B

$$C = 45 \text{ balls}$$
$$A = 2 \cdot C = 2 \cdot 45 = 90 \text{ balls}$$
$$B = 3 \cdot C = 3 \cdot 45 = 135 \text{ balls}$$

Try again

Replace these values in F1 (s)

$$F_1(s) = A^2 + B^2 = 13 \cdot C^2$$
$$= 90^2 + 135^2 = 13 \text{x} 45^2 = 26325$$

Solution 1:

> A = green balls: 90
>
> B = yellow balls 135
>
> C = purple balls 45

> A + B + C
>
> 90 + 135 + 45 = 270 Balls

The second approach to

> $\zeta(s) = 1.2^2 + 3.4^2 = 13$
>
> $A = 1.2 \cdot C$
>
> $B = 3.4 \cdot C$

The values of A, B

> C = 45 balls
>
> $A = 1.2 \cdot C = 1.2 \cdot 45 = 54$ balls
>
> $B = 3.4 \cdot C = 3.4 \cdot 45 = 153$ balls

Try again

Replace these values in F1 (s)

> $F_1(s) = A^2 + B^2 = 13.C^2$
>
> $= 54^2 + 153^2 = 13 \times 45^2 = 26325$

Solution 2:

> A = green balls 54
>
> B = yellow balls 153
>
> C = purple balls 45

A + B + C

54 + 153 + 45 = 252 Balls

The third approach to

$$\zeta(s) = 0.2^2 + 3.6^2 = 13$$
$$A = 0.2 \cdot C$$
$$B = 3.6 \cdot C$$

The values of A, B

C = 45 ball

A = 0.2 · C = 0.2 · 45 = 9 balls

B = 3.6 · C = 3.6 · 45 = 162 balls

Try again

Replace these values in F1 (s)

$$F_1(s) = A^2 + B^2 = 13 \cdot C^2$$
$$= 9^2 + 162^2 = 13 \cdot 45^2 = 26325$$

Solution 3:

A = green balls: 9

B = yellow balls 162

C = purple balls 45

A + B + C

9 + 162 + 45 = 216 Balls

Solution 1:

> A = green balls: 90
>
> B = yellow balls 135
>
> C = purple balls 45

Solution 2:

> A = green balls: 54
>
> B = yellow balls 153
>
> C = purple balls 45

Solution 3:

> A = green balls: 9
>
> B = yellow balls 162
>
> C = purple balls 45

....

~~~~~~~//////~~~~~~~

*) The balls are three different colors, green, yellow, purple green, and yellow balls are squared then sum of both, it's equal to powers 3 of purple balls

Given: 170 purple balls

How many balls of each color?

Solve

We put

A = green balls

B = yellow balls

C = purple balls

We have

$$F_1(s) = A^2 + B^2 = C^3$$

Rewrite

$$F_1(s) = A^2 + B^2 = C \cdot C^2$$

Back to problem Fermat Wiles equaion

$$x^n + y^n = c \cdot z^n$$

Applying the popular method, with $n = 2$

$$\zeta(s) = r^n + s^n = c$$

$$s = \sqrt[n]{c - r^n}$$
$$r = \sqrt[n]{c - s^n}$$
$$\zeta(s) = c \ \& \ \zeta(c) = 0$$
$$x = r \cdot z = \sqrt[n]{c - s^n} \cdot z$$
$$y = s \cdot z = \sqrt[n]{c - r^n} \cdot z$$

$$n \rightarrow \infty$$

The values of A, B, c

$$\zeta(s) = c \text{ and } \zeta(c) = 0$$

Replace C by c

$$A^2 + B^2 = c \cdot C^2$$

Find the values of r, s

$$C = c = 170$$

$$\zeta(s) = r^2 + s^2 = c = 170$$
$$1^2 + 13^2 = 170$$
$$7^2 + 11^2 = 170$$

$$A = r \cdot C$$
$$B = s \cdot C$$

The first approach to

$$\zeta(s) = 1^2 + 13^2 = 170$$
$$A = 1 \cdot C$$
$$B = 13 \cdot C$$

The values of A, B

$$C = 170 \text{ balls}$$
$$A = 1 \cdot C = 1 \cdot 170 = 170 \text{ balls}$$
$$B = 3 \cdot C = 13 \cdot 170 = 2210 \text{ balls}$$

Try again

Replace these values in F1 (s)

$$F_1(s) = A^2 + B^2 = C^3$$
$$= 170^2 + 2210^2 = 170^3 = 4913000$$

Solution 1:

A = green balls: 170

B = yellow balls 2210

C = purple balls 170

A + B + C

170 + 2210 + 170 = 2550 Balls

The second approach to

$$\zeta(s) = 7^2 + 11^2 = 170$$
$$A = 7 \cdot C$$
$$B = 11 \cdot C$$

The values of A, B

C = 170 balls

$$A = 7 \cdot C = 7 \cdot 170 = 1190 \text{ balls}$$
$$B = 11 \cdot C = 11 \cdot 170 = 1870 \text{ balls}$$

Try again

Replace these values in F1 (s)

$$F_1(s) = A^2 + B^2 = C^3$$
$$= 1190^2 + 1870^2 = 170^3 = 4913000$$

Solution 2:

A = green balls: 1190

B = yellow balls 1870

C = purple balls 170

A + B + C

1190 + 1870 + 170 = 3230 Balls

Solution 1:

A = green balls: 170

B = yellow balls 2210

C = purple balls 170

Solution 2:

A = green balls: 1190

B = yellow balls 1870

C = purple balls 170

….

~~~~~~~//////~~~~~~

EXERCISES

*) There are 240 candies in the candy box with 3 different colors: blue, yellow, and purple
The square of blue and yellow candies then sum of both is equal to the multiple of 17 by the square of purple candies

How many candies in candy box?
How many candies of each color?

*) There are 350 candies in candy box, with 3 different colors: blue, yellow and purple
The square of blue, and yellow candies, then sum of both is equal to multiple of 20 by the square purple candies

How many candies in candy box, which more than?
How many candies of each color?

*) There are 350 candies in candy box, with 3 different colors: blue, yellow and purple

The square of blue, and yellow candies, then sum of both is equal to multiple of 25 by the square purple candies

How many candies in candy box, which more than?
How many candies of each color?

*) There are 480 candies in candy box, with 3 different colors: blue, yellow and purple
The square of blue, and yellow candies, then sum of both is equal to multiple of 65 by the square purple candies

How many candies in candy box, which more than?
How many candies of each color?

*) Find the values of x, y of the Diophantine equation
$x^2 + y^2 = 313^3$
(x, y are the whole numbers)

*) Find the values of x, y of the Diophantine equation
$x^2 + y^2 = 970^3$
(x, y are the whole numbers)

*) There are 370 candies in candy box, with 3 different colors: blue, yellow and purple
The square of blue, and yellow candies, then sum of both is equal to multiple of 29 by the square purple candies

How many candies in candy box, which more than?
How many candies of each color?

*) There are 1000 candies in candy box, with 3 different colors: blue, yellow and purple
The square of blue, and yellow candies, then sum of both is equal to multiple of 45 by the square purple candies

How many candies in candy box, which more than?
How many candies of each color?

*) Inside the balls box, with three different colors of green, yellow, and purple, the square of green, and yellow balls, then sum of both is equal to the 3rd power of purple balls
Given: 90 purple balls

How many balls in the box more than?
How many balls of each color?

*) In the balls box, with three different colors, green, yellow, purple, the square of green, and yellow balls, then sum of both is equal to the 3rd power of purple balls

Given: 113 purple balls

How many balls in the box more than?
How many balls of each color?

*) In the balls box, with three different colors, green, yellow, purple, the square of green, and yellow balls, then sum of both is equal to the 3rd power of purple balls

Given: 130 purple balls

How many balls in the box more than?
How many balls of each color?

*) In the balls box, with three different colors, green, yellow, purple, the square of green, and yellow balls, then sum of both is equal to the 3rd power of purple balls

Given: 185 purple balls

How many balls in the box more than?
How many balls of each color?

*) In the balls box, with three different colors, green, yellow, purple, the square of green, and yellow balls, then sum of both is equal to the 3rd power of purple balls

Given: 317 purple balls

How many balls in the box more than?
How many balls of each color?

*) In the balls box, with three different colors, green, yellow, purple, the square of green, and yellow balls, then sum of both is equal to the 3rd power of purple balls

Given: 2050 purple balls

How many balls in the box more than?
How many balls of each color?

*) Find the values of x, y, z of the Diophantine equation

$x^2 + y^2 = 20z^2$

(x, y, z are the whole numbers)

*) Find the values of x, y, z of the Diophantine equation

$x^2 + y^2 = 4z^2$

(x, y, z are the whole numbers)

*) Find the values of x, y, z of the Diophantine equation

$x^2 + y^2 = 17z^2$

(x, y, z are the whole numbers)

*) Find the values of x, y, z of the Diophantine equation

$x^2 + y^2 = 18z^2$

(x, y, z are the whole numbers)

*) Find the values of x, y, z of the Diophantine equation

$x^2 + y^2 = 9z^2$

(x, y, z are the whole numbers)

*) Find the values of x, y of the Diophantine equation

$5x^2 - y^2 = 4$

(x, y are the whole numbers)

*) Find the values of x, y of the Diophantine equation

$8x^2 - y^2 = 4$

(x, y are the whole numbers)

*) Find the values of x, y of the Diophantine equation

$18x^2 - y^2 = 9$

(x, y are the whole numbers)

FERMAT-WILES EQUATION TO EXPAND

$$v^n + x^n + y^n = d \cdot z^n$$

The Diophantine eqution or Fermat Wiles equation
$x^n + y^n = c \cdot z^n$ it's not difficult

Similarly Fermat-Wiles Equation, just add "v", we expand such as the following form
$$v^n + x^n + y^n = d \cdot z^n$$

Applying the popular method
$$\zeta(s) = r^n + s^n = c$$

$$s = \sqrt[n]{c - r^n}$$
$$r = \sqrt[n]{c - s^n}$$
$$\zeta(s) = c \ \& \ \zeta(c) = 0$$
$$x = r \cdot z = \sqrt[n]{c - s^n \cdot z}$$
$$y = s \cdot z = \sqrt[n]{c - r^n \cdot z}$$

$$n \rightarrow \infty$$

Expand a term as follows, we get

$$v^n + x^n + y^n = d \cdot z^n$$

Or

$$A^n + B^n + C^n = d \cdot D^n$$

The values of d

$$\zeta(s) = d \text{ and } \zeta(d) = 0$$

$$\zeta(s) = r^2 + s^2 + t^2 = d$$

The values of A, B, C, D

$$A = r \cdot D$$

$$B = s \cdot D$$

$$C = t \cdot D$$

APPLICATION

*) There are 220 balls, with four different colors, red, green, yellow and purple.

If the second power red, green, and yellow balls, then sum all of three is equal to multiple of 38 by the second power of purple balls

How many balls of each color?

Solve

We put

A= red ball

B = green ball

C = yellow ball

D = purple ball

We have

$$F_1(s) = A + B + C + D = 220$$

And

$$F_2(s) = A^2 + B^2 + C^2 = 38 \cdot D^2$$

Applying the popular method

$$\zeta(s) = r^n + s^n = c$$

$$s = \sqrt[n]{c - r^n}$$
$$r = \sqrt[n]{c - s^n}$$
$$\zeta(s) = c \ \& \ \zeta(c) = 0$$
$$x = r \cdot z = \sqrt[n]{c - s^n \cdot z}$$
$$y = s \cdot z = \sqrt[n]{c - r^n \cdot z}$$

$$n \to \infty$$

Expanded method as follows

$$\zeta(s) = d \text{ and } \zeta(d) = 0$$
$$\zeta(s) = r^2 + s^2 + t^2 = 38$$

The values of unknouwns

$$A = r \cdot D$$
$$B = s \cdot D$$
$$C = t \cdot D$$

The values of r, s, t

$$\zeta(s) = 2^2 + 3^2 + 5^2 = 38$$

The value of D

$$D = \frac{220}{r + s + t + 1} = \frac{220}{11} = 20$$

The value of A

$$A = r \cdot D$$
$$A = 2 \cdot 20 = 40$$

The value of B

$$B = s \cdot D$$
$$B = 3 \cdot 20 = 60$$

The value of C

$$C = t \cdot D$$
$$C = 5 \cdot 20 = 100$$

Try again

Replace these values into F1 (s) and F2 (s)

$$F_1(s) = A + B + C + D = 220$$
$$= 40 + 60 + 100 + 20 = 220$$

$$F_2(s) = A^2 + B^2 + C^2 = 38 \cdot D^2$$
$$F_2(s) = 40^2 + 60^2 + 100^2 = 38 \cdot 20^2 = 15200$$

Solution:

A = red ball = 40

B = green ball = 60

C = yellow ball = 100

D = purple ball = 20

*) There are 255 balls, with four different colors, red, green, yellow and purple.

If the second power red, green, and yellow balls, then sum all of three is equal to multiple of 78 by the second power of purple balls

How many balls of each color?

Solve

We put

A = red ball

B = green ball

C = yellow ball

D = purple ball

We have

$$F_1(s) = A + B + C + D = 225$$

And

$$F_2(s) = A^2 + B^2 + C^2 = 78 \cdot D^2$$

Applying the popular method

$$\zeta(s) = r^n + s^n = c$$

$$s = \sqrt[n]{c - r^n}$$
$$r = \sqrt[n]{c - s^n}$$

$$\zeta(s) = c \ \& \ \zeta(c) = 0$$
$$x = r \cdot z = ^n\sqrt{c - s^n \cdot z}$$

$$y = s \cdot z = ^n\sqrt{c - r^n \cdot z}$$

$$n \to \infty$$

Expanded method as follows

$$\zeta(s) = d \text{ and } \zeta(d) = 0$$
$$\zeta(s) = r^2 + s^2 + t^2 = 78$$

The values of unknouwns

$$A = r \cdot D$$
$$B = s \cdot D$$
$$C = t \cdot D$$

The values of r, s, t

$$\zeta(s) = 2^2 + 5^2 + 7^2 = 78$$

The value of D

$$D = \frac{225}{r + s + t + 1} = \frac{255}{15} = 17$$

The value of A

$$A = r \cdot D$$
$$A = 2 \cdot 17 = 34$$

The value of B

$$B = s \cdot D$$
$$B = 5 \cdot 17 = 85$$

The value of C

$$C = t \cdot D$$
$$C = 7 \cdot 17 = 119$$

Try again

Replace these values in F1 (s) and F2 (s)

$$F_1(s) = A + B + C + D = 255$$
$$= 34 + 85 + 119 + 17 = 255$$

$$F_2(s) = A^2 + B^2 + C^2 = 78 \cdot D^2$$
$$F_2(s) = 34^2 + 85^2 + 119^2 = 78 \cdot 17^2 = 22542$$

Solution:

A = red ball = 34
B = green ball = 85
C = yellow ball = 119
D = purple ball = 17

*) There are 250 balls, with four different colors, red, green, yellow and purple.

If the second power red, green, and yellow balls, then sum all of three is equal to multiple of 29 by the second power of purple balls

How many balls of each color?

Solve

We put

A = red ball

B = green ball

C = yellow ball

D = purple ball

We have

$$F_1(s) = A + B + C + D = 250$$

And

$$F_2(s) = A^2 + B^2 + C^2 = 29 \cdot D^2$$

Applying the popular method

$$\zeta(s) = r^n + s^n = c$$

$$s = \sqrt[n]{c - r^n}$$
$$r = \sqrt[n]{c - s^n}$$

$$\zeta(s) = c \ \& \ \zeta(c) = 0$$
$$x = r \cdot z = \sqrt[n]{c - s^n \cdot z}$$
$$y = s \cdot z = \sqrt[n]{c - r^n \cdot z}$$
$$n \to \infty$$

Expanded method as follows

$$\zeta(s) = d \text{ and } \zeta(d) = 0$$
$$\zeta(s) = r^2 + s^2 + t^2 = 29$$

The values of unknouwns

$$A = r \cdot D$$
$$B = s \cdot D$$
$$C = t \cdot D$$

The values of r, s, t

$$\zeta(s) = r^2 + s^2 + t^2 = 29$$
$$\zeta(s)_1 = 2^2 + 3^2 + 4^2 = 29$$
$$\zeta(s)_2 = 1.2^2 + 1.6^2 + 5^2 = 29$$
$$\zeta(s)_3 = 1.2^2 + 3.4^2 + 4^2 = 29$$
$$\zeta(s)_4 = 0.2^2 + 3.6^2 + 4^2 = 29$$
$$\zeta(s)_5 = 0.8^2 + 4.4^2 + 3^2 = 29$$

...

Substitution the values of $\zeta(s) = r^2 + s^2 + t^2 = 29$

Into:

$$A = r \cdot D$$
$$B = s \cdot D$$
$$C = t \cdot D$$

We have 5 answers

The answer 1

$$\zeta(s)_1 = 2^2 + 3^2 + 4^2 = 29$$

The value of D

$$D = \frac{250}{r+s+t+1} = \frac{250}{10} = 25$$

The value of A

$$A = r \cdot D$$
$$A = 2 \cdot 25 = 50$$

The value of B

$$B = s \cdot D$$
$$B = 3 \cdot 25 = 75$$

The value of C

$$C = t \cdot D$$
$$C = 4 \cdot 25 = 100$$

Try again

Replace these values into F1 (s) and F2 (s)

$$F_1(s) = A + B + C + D = 250$$
$$= 50 + 75 + 100 + 25 = 250$$

$$F_2(s) = A^2 + B^2 + C^2 = 29 \cdot D^2$$
$$F_2(s) = 50^2 + 75^2 + 100^2 = 29 \cdot 25^2 = 18125$$

The answer 2

$$\zeta(s)_2 = 1.2^2 + 1.6^2 + 5^2 = 29$$

The value of D

$$D = \frac{250}{r + s + t + 1} = \frac{250}{8,8} = 28,40909090909090$$

D is not whole number, in this case we do not get

The answer 3

$$\zeta(s)_3 = 1.2^2 + 3.4^2 + 4^2 = 29$$

The value of D

$$D = \frac{250}{r+s+t+1} = \frac{250}{.9,6} = 26,041666666666666$$

We do not get

The answer 4

$$\zeta(s)_4 = 0.2^2 + 3.6^2 + 4^2 = 29$$

The value of D

$$D = \frac{250}{r+s+t+1} = \frac{250}{8,8} = 28,40909090909090$$

We do not get

The answer 5

$$\zeta(s)_5 = 0.8^2 + 4.4^2 + 3^2 = 29$$

The value of D

$$D = \frac{250}{r+s+t+1} = \frac{250}{9,2} = 27,17391304347826086 95$$

We do not get

Solution

A= red ball = 50

B = green ball = 75

C = yellow ball = 100

D = purple ball = 25

~~~~~~~//////~~~~~~~

*) There are 255 balls, with four different colors, red, green, yellow and purple.

If the second power red, green, and yellow balls, then sum all of three is equal to multiple of 98 by the second power of purple balls

How many balls of each color?

Solve

We put

A = red ball

B = green ball

C = yellow ball

D = purple ball

We have

$$F_1(s) = A + B + C + D = 255$$

And

$$F_2(s) = A^2 + B^2 + C^2 = 98 \cdot D^2$$

Applying the popular method

$$\zeta(s) = r^n + s^n = c$$
$$s = \sqrt[n]{c - r^n}$$
$$r = \sqrt[n]{c - s^n}$$
$$\zeta(s) = c \ \& \ \zeta(c) = 0$$

$$x = r \cdot z = \sqrt[n]{c - s^n \cdot z}$$
$$y = s \cdot z = \sqrt[n]{c - r^n \cdot z}$$

$$n \rightarrow \infty$$

Expanded method as follows

$$\zeta(s) = d \text{ and } \zeta(d) = 0$$
$$\zeta(s) = r^2 + s^2 + t^2 = 98$$

The values of unknouwns

$$A = r \cdot D$$
$$B = s \cdot D$$
$$C = t \cdot D$$

The values of r, s, t

$$\zeta(s) = r^2 + s^2 + t^2 = 98$$
$$\zeta(s)_1 = 1^2 + 4^2 + 9^2 = 98$$
$$\zeta(s)_2 = 3^2 + 5^2 + 8^2 = 98$$

...

Substitution the values of $\zeta(s) = r^2 + s^2 + t^2 = 98$
Into:

$$A = r \cdot D$$
$$B = s \cdot D$$
$$C = t \cdot D$$

We get 2 answers

The answer 1

$$\zeta(s)_1 = 1^2 + 4^2 + 9^2 = 98$$

The value of D

$$D = \frac{255}{r+s+t+1} = \frac{255}{15} = 17$$

The value of A

A = r · D

A = 1 · 17 = 17

The value of B

B = s · D

B = 4 · 17 = 68

The value of C

C = t · D

C = 9 · 17 = 153

Try again

Replace these values into F1 (s) and F2 (s)

$F_1(s) = A + B + C + D = 255$

$= 17 + 68 + 153 + 17 = 255$

$F_2(s) = A^2 + B^2 + C^2 = 98 \cdot D^2$

$F_2(s) = 17^2 + 68^2 + 153^2 = 98 \cdot 17^2 = 28322$

The answer 2

$\zeta(s)_2 = 3^2 + 5^2 + 8^2 = 98$

The value of D

$$D = \frac{255}{r+s+t+1} = \frac{255}{17} = 15$$

The value of A

$$A = r \cdot D$$
$$A = 3 \cdot 15 = 45$$

The value of B

$$B = s \cdot D$$
$$B = 5 \cdot 15 = 75$$

The value of C

$$C = t \cdot D$$
$$C = 8 \cdot 15 = 120$$

Try again

Replace these values in F1 (s) and F2 (s)

$$F_1(s) = A + B + C + D = 255$$
$$= 45 + 75 + 120 + 15 = 255$$

$$F_2(s) = A^2 + B^2 + C^2 = 98 \cdot D^2$$
$$F_2(s) = 45^2 + 75^2 + 120^2 = 98 \cdot 15^2 = 22050$$

Solution 1

A= red ball = 17
B = green ball = 68
C = yellow ball = 153
D = purple ball = 17

Solution2

A= red ball = 45

B = green ball = 75

C = yellow ball = 120

D = purple ball = 15

*) There are 250 balls, with four different colors, red, green, yellow and purple.

If the second power red, green, and yellow balls, then sum all of three is equal to multiple of 29 by the second power of purple balls

How many balls of each color?

Solve

We put

A= red ball

B = green ball

C = yellow ball

D = purple ball

We have

$F_1(s) = A + B + C + D = 297$

And

$$F_2(s) = A^2 + B^2 + C^2 = 38 \cdot D^2$$

Aplying popular method

$$\zeta(s) = r^n + s^n = c$$

$$s = \sqrt[n]{c - r^n}$$
$$r = \sqrt[n]{c - s}$$
$$\zeta(s) = c \ \& \ \zeta(c) = 0$$

$$x = r \cdot z = \sqrt[n]{c - s^n \cdot z}$$
$$y = s \cdot z = \sqrt[n]{c - r^n \cdot z}$$

$$n \to \infty$$

Expanded method as follows

$$\zeta(s) = d \text{ and } \zeta(d) = 0$$
$$\zeta(s) = r^2 + s^2 + t^2 = 38$$

The values of unknouwns

$$A = r \cdot D$$
$$B = s \cdot D$$
$$C = t \cdot D$$

The values of r, s, t

$$\zeta(s) = r^2 + s^2 + t^2 = 38$$
$$\zeta(s)_1 = 1^2 + 1^2 + 6^2 = 38$$
$$\zeta(s)_2 = 1.2^2 + 3.4^2 + 5^2 = 38$$

$$\zeta(s)_3 = 2^2 + 3^2 + 5^2 = 38$$
$$\zeta(s)_4 = 3.6^2 + 0.2^2 + 5^2 = 38$$

...

Substitution the values of $\zeta(s) = r^2 + s^2 + t^2 = 38$
Into:

$$A = r \cdot D$$
$$B = s \cdot D$$
$$C = t \cdot D$$

We get 4 answers

The answer 1

$$\zeta(s)_1 = 1^2 + 1^2 + 6^2 = 38$$

The value of D

$$D = \frac{297}{r+s+t+1} = \frac{297}{9} = 33$$

The value of A

$$A = r \cdot D$$
$$A = 1 \cdot 33 = 33$$

The value of B

$$B = s \cdot D$$
$$B = 1 \cdot 33 = 33$$

The value of C

$$C = t \cdot D$$
$$C = 6 \cdot 33 = 198$$

Try again

Replace these values into F1 (s) and F2 (s)

$$F_1(s) = A + B + C + D = 297$$
$$= 33 + 33 + 198 + 33 = 297$$

$$F_2(s) = A^2 + B^2 + C^2 = 29 \cdot D^2$$
$$F_2(s) = 33^2 + 33^2 + 198^2 = 38 \cdot 33^2 = 41382$$

The answer 2

$$\zeta(s)_2 = 1.2^2 + 3.4^2 + 5^2 = 38$$

The value of D

$$D = \frac{297}{r + s + t + 1} = \frac{297}{10.6} = 28,11320754716981$$

we do not get

The answer 3

$$\zeta(s)_3 = 2^2 + 3^2 + 5^2 = 38$$

The value of D

$$D = \frac{297}{r + s + t + 1} = \frac{297}{11} = 27$$

The value of A

$$A = r \cdot D$$
$$A = 2 \cdot 27 = 54$$

The value of B

$$B = s \cdot D$$
$$B = 3 \cdot 27 = 81$$

The value of C

$$C = t \cdot D$$
$$C = 5 \cdot 27 = 135$$

Try again

Replace these values into F1 (s) and F2 (s)

$$F_1(s) = A + B + C + D = 297$$
$$= 54 + 81 + 135 + 27 = 297$$

$$F_2(s) = A^2 + B^2 + C^2 = 29 \cdot D^2$$
$$F_2(s) = 54^2 + 81^2 + 135^2 = 38 \cdot 27^2 = 27702$$

The answer 4

$$\zeta(s)_4 = 3.6^2 + 0.2^2 + 5^2 = 38$$

The value of D

$$D = \frac{297}{r + s + t + 1} = \frac{297}{9.8} = 30,30612244897959183$$

We do not get

Solution 1

$$A = \text{red ball} = 33$$
$$B = \text{green ball} = 33$$
$$C = \text{yellow ball} = 198$$
$$D = \text{purple ball} = 33$$

Solution 2

A= red ball = 54

B = green ball = 81

C = yellow ball = 135

D = purple ball = 27

––––––––––––––––––

*) In the balls box, with 4 different colors, red, green, yellow, purple

If the second power red, green, and yellow balls, then sum all of three is equal to 3rd powers of purple balls

Given: 78 purple balls

How many balls of each color?

Solve

We put

A= red ball

B = green ball

C = yellow ball

D = purple ball

We have

$$F_1(s) = A^2 + B^2 + C^2 = D^3$$

Rewrite

$$F_1(s) = A^2 + B^2 + C^2 = D \cdot D^2$$

Back to Fermat Wiles equaion

$$x^n + y^n = c \cdot z^n$$

Applying the popular method, with n = 2

$$\zeta(s) = r^n + s^n = c$$

$$s = \sqrt{c - r}$$
$$r = \sqrt[n]{c - s^n}$$
$$\zeta(s) = c \;\&\; \zeta(c) = 0$$
$$x = r \cdot z = \sqrt[n]{c - s^n} \cdot z$$
$$y = s \cdot z = \sqrt[n]{c - r^n} \cdot z$$

$$n \rightarrow \infty$$

The values of A, B, C, d

$$\zeta(s) = d \text{ and } \zeta(d) = 0$$

Replace D by d

$$F_1(s) = A^2 + B^2 + C^2 = d \cdot D^2$$

Find the values of r, s, t

$$D = d = 78$$
$$\zeta(s) = r^2 + s^2 + t^2 = 78$$
$$2^2 + 5^2 + 7^2 = 78$$

The value of D = 78

The value of A

$$A = r \cdot D$$
$$A = 2 \cdot 78 = 156$$

The value of B

$$B = s \cdot D$$
$$B = 5 \cdot 78 = 390$$

The value of C

$$C = t \cdot D$$
$$C = 7 \cdot 78 = 546$$

Try again

Replace these values into F1 (s)

$$F_1(s) = A^2 + B^2 + C^2 = D^3$$
$$F_1(s) = 156^2 + 390^2 + 546^2 = 78^3 = 474552$$

Solution

Bucket balls = 1170 balls

A = red ball = 156

B = green ball = 390

C = yellow ball = 546

D = purple ball = 78

_____

*) In the balls box, with 4 different colors, red, green, yellow, purple

If the second power red, green, and yellow balls, then sum all of three is equal to multiple of 38 by the square purple balls

Given: 35 purple balls

How many balls of each color?

Solve

We put

> A= red ball
>
> B = green ball
>
> C = yellow ball
>
> D = purple ball

We have

$$F(s) = A^2 + B^2 + C^2 = 38 \cdot D^2$$

Applying popular method

$$\zeta(s) = r^n + s^n = c$$

$$s = \sqrt[n]{c - r^n}$$
$$r = \sqrt[n]{c - s^n}$$

$$\zeta(s) = c \ \& \ \zeta(c) = 0$$

$$x = r \cdot z = \sqrt[n]{c - s^n \cdot z}$$
$$y = s \cdot z = \sqrt[n]{c - r^n \cdot z}$$

$$n \rightarrow \infty$$

Expanded method as follows

$$\zeta(s) = d \text{ and } \zeta(d) = 0$$
$$\zeta(s) = r^2 + s^2 + t^2 = 38$$

The values of unknouwns

> A = r \cdot D
>
> B = s \cdot D
>
> C = t \cdot D

The values of r, s, t

$$\zeta(s) = r^2 + s^2 + t^2 = 38$$
$$\zeta(s)_1 = 1^2 + 1^2 + 6^2 = 38$$
$$\zeta(s)_2 = 1.2^2 + 3.4^2 + 5^2 = 38$$
$$\zeta(s)_3 = 2^2 + 3^2 + 5^2 = 38$$
$$\zeta(s)_4 = 3.6^2 + 0.2^2 + 5^2 = 38$$

...

Substitution the values of $\zeta(s) = r^2 + s^2 + t^2 = d = 38$ for solution of the Diophantine equation

$$F(s) = A^2 + B^2 + C^2 = 38 \cdot D^2$$

The first approach to

$$\zeta(s)_1 = 1^2 + 1^2 + 6^2 = 38$$

$$A = r \cdot D$$
$$B = s \cdot D$$
$$C = t \cdot D$$

The values of A, B, C

$$D = 35 \text{ balls}$$
$$A = 1 \cdot D = 1 \cdot 35 = 35 \text{ balls}$$
$$B = 1 \cdot D = 1 \cdot 35 = 35 \text{ balls}$$
$$C = 6 \cdot D = 6 \cdot 35 = 210 \text{ balls}$$

Try again

Replace these values into F(s)

$$F(s) = A^2 + B^2 + C^2 = 38 \cdot D^2$$
$$F(s) = 35^2 + 35^2 + 210^2 = 38 \cdot 35^2 = 46550$$

Solution 1:

> A= red ball = 35
>
> B = green ball = 35
>
> C = yellow ball = 210
>
> D = purple ball = 35

The second approach to

> $\zeta(s)_2 = 1.2^2 + 3.4^2 + 5^2 = 38$
>
> $A = r \cdot D$
>
> $B = s \cdot D$
>
> $C = t \cdot D$

The values of A, B, C

> D = 35 balls
>
> A = 1.2 · D = 1.2 · 35 = 42 balls
>
> B = 3.4 · D = 3.4 · 35 = 119 balls
>
> C = 5 · D = 5 · 35 = 175 balls

Try again

Replace these values into F(s)

> $F(s) = A^2 + B^2 + C^2 = 38 \cdot D^2$
>
> $F(s) = 42^2 + 119^2 + 175^2 = 38 \cdot 35^2 = 46550$

Solution 2:

> A= red ball = 42
>
> B = green ball = 119

C = yellow ball = 175

D = purple ball = 35

The third approach to

$\zeta(s)_3 = 2^2 + 3^2 + 5^2 = 38$

A = r · D

B = s · D

C = t · D

The values of A, B, C

D = 35 balls

A = 2 · D = 2 · 35 = 70 balls

B = 3 · D = 3 · 35 = 105 balls

C = 5 · D = 5 · 35 = 175 balls

Try again

Replace these values into F(s)

$F(s) = A^2 + B^2 + C^2 = 38 \cdot D^2$

$F(s) = 70^2 + 105^2 + 175^2 = 38 \cdot 35^2 = 46550$

Solution 3:

A = red ball = 70

B = green ball = 105

C = yellow ball = 175

D = purple ball = 35

The 4th approach to

$$\zeta(s)_4 = 3.6^2 + 0.2^2 + 5^2 = 38$$
$$A = r \cdot D$$
$$B = s \cdot D$$
$$C = t \cdot D$$

The values of A, B, C

$$D = 35 \text{ balls}$$
$$A = 3.6 \cdot D = 3.6 \cdot 35 = 126 \text{ balls}$$
$$B = 0.2 \cdot D = 0.2 \cdot 35 = 7 \text{ balls}$$
$$C = 5 \cdot D = 5 \cdot 35 = 175 \text{ balls}$$

Try again

Replace these values into F(s)

$$F(s) = A^2 + B^2 + C^2 = 38 \cdot D^2$$
$$F(s) = 126^2 + 7^2 + 175^2 = 38 \cdot 35^2 = 46550$$

Solution 4:

$$A = \text{red ball} = 126$$
$$B = \text{green ball} = 7$$
$$C = \text{yellow ball} = 175$$
$$D = \text{purple ball} = 35$$

Solution 1:

$$A = \text{red ball} = 35$$
$$B = \text{green ball} = 35$$
$$C = \text{yellow ball} = 210$$
$$D = \text{purple ball} = 35$$

Solution 2:

> A= red ball = 42
>
> B = green ball = 119
>
> C = yellow ball = 175
>
> D = purple ball = 35

Solution 3:

> A= red ball = 70
>
> B = green ball = 105
>
> C = yellow ball = 175
>
> D = purple ball = 35

Solution 4:

> A= red ball = 126
>
> B = green ball = 7
>
> C = yellow ball = 175
>
> D = purple ball = 35

….

~~~~~~~//////~~~~~~

*) In the balls box, with 4 different colors, red, green, yellow, purple

If the second power red, green, and yellow balls, then sum all of three is equal to 3rd powers of purple balls

Given: 194 purple balls

How many balls of each color?

Solve

We put

$$A = \text{red ball}$$
$$B = \text{green ball}$$
$$C = \text{yellow ball}$$
$$D = \text{purple ball}$$

We have

$$F_1(s) = A^2 + B^2 + C^2 = D^3$$

Rewrite

$$F_1(s) = A^2 + B^2 + C^2 = D \cdot D^2$$

Back to Fermat Wiles equaion

$$x^n + y^n = c \cdot z^n$$

Applying the popular method, $n = 2$

$$\zeta(s) = r^n + s^n = c$$

$$s = \sqrt[n]{c - r^n}$$
$$r = \sqrt[n]{c - s^n}$$
$$\zeta(s) = c \ \& \ \zeta(c) = 0$$
$$x = r \cdot z = \sqrt[n]{c - s^n \cdot z}$$
$$y = s \cdot z = \sqrt[n]{c - r^n \cdot z}$$

$$n \to \infty$$

The values of A, B, C, d

$$\zeta(s) = d \text{ and } \zeta(d) = 0$$

Replace D by d

$$F_1(s) = A^2 + B^2 + C^2 = d \cdot D^2$$

Find the values of r, s, t

$$D = d = 194$$

$$\zeta(s) = r^2 + s^2 + t^2 = d = 194$$
$$\zeta(s)_1 = 3^2 + 8^2 + 11^2 = 194$$
$$\zeta(s)_2 = 1^2 + 7^2 + 12^2 = 194$$
$$\zeta(s)_3 = 3^2 + 4^2 + 13^2 = 194$$

The first approach to

$$\zeta(s)_1 = 3^2 + 8^2 + 11^2 = 194$$
$$A = r \cdot D$$
$$B = s \cdot D$$
$$C = t \cdot D$$

The values of A, B, C

$$D = 194 \text{ balls}$$
$$A = 3 \cdot D = 3 \cdot 194 = 582 \text{ balls}$$
$$B = 8 \cdot D = 8 \cdot 194 = 1552 \text{ balls}$$
$$C = 11 \cdot D = 11 \cdot 194 = 2134 \text{ balls}$$

Try again

Replace these values into F(s)

$$F(s) = A^2 + B^2 + C^2 = 194^3$$
$$F(s) = 582^2 + 1552^2 + 2134^2 = 194^3 = 7301384$$

Solution 1:

A= red ball = 582

B = green ball = 1552

C = yellow ball = 2134

D = purple ball = 194

The second approach to

$$\zeta(s)_2 = 1^2 + 7^2 + 12^2 = 194$$
$$A = r \cdot D$$
$$B = s \cdot D$$
$$C = t \cdot D$$

The values of A, B, C

D = 194 balls

$A = 1 \cdot D = 1 \cdot 194 = 194$ balls

$B = 7 \cdot D = 7 \cdot 194 = 1358$ balls

$C = 12 \cdot D = 12 \cdot 194 = 2328$ balls

Try again

Replace these values in F(s)

$$F(s) = A^2 + B^2 + C^2 = 194^3$$
$$F(s) = 194^2 + 1358^2 + 2328^2 = 194^3 = 7301384$$

Solution 2:

A= red ball = 194

B = green ball = 1358

C = yellow ball = 2328

D = purple ball = 194

The third approach to

$\zeta(s)_3 = 3^2 + 4^2 + 13^2 = 194$

A = r · D

B = s · D

C = t · D

The values of A, B, C

D = 194 balls

A = 3 · D = 3 · 194 = 582 balls

B = 4 · D = 4 · 194 = 776 balls

C = 13 · D = 13 · 194 = 2522 balls

Try again

Replace these values into F(s)

$F(s) = A^2 + B^2 + C^2 = 194^3$

$F(s) = 582^2 + 776^2 + 2522^2 = 194^3 = 7301384$

Solution 3:

A= red ball = 582

B = green ball = 776

C = yellow ball = 2522

D = purple ball = 194

Solution 1:

> A= red ball = 582
>
> B = green ball = 1552
>
> C = yellow ball = 2134
>
> D = purple ball = 194

Solution 2:

> A= red ball = 194
>
> B = green ball = 1358
>
> C = yellow ball = 2328
>
> D = purple ball = 194

Solution 3:

> A= red ball = 582
>
> B = green ball = 776
>
> C = yellow ball = 2522
>
> D = purple ball = 194

EXERCISES

*) There are 518 balls, with four different colors, red, green, yellow, purple.
If square of the red, green, and yellow balls, then sum all of three is equal to multiple of 14 by the square purple balls

How many balls of each color?

*) There are 120 balls, with four different colors, red, green, yellow, purple.
If square of the red, green, and yellow balls, then sum all of three is equal to multiple of 49 by the square purple balls

How many balls of each color?

*) There are 86 balls, with four different colors, red, green, yellow, purple.
If square of the red, green, and yellow balls, then sum all of three is equal to multiple of 20 by the square purple balls

How many balls of each color?

*) There are 168 balls, with four different colors, red, green, yellow, purple.

If square of the red, green, and yellow balls, then sum all of three is equal to multiple of 21 by the square purple balls

How many balls of each color?

*) There are 544 balls, with four different colors, red, green, yellow, purple.

If square of the red, green, and yellow balls, then sum all of three is equal to multiple of 19 by the square purple balls

How many balls of each color?

*) There are 120 balls, with four different colors, red, green, yellow, purple.

If square of the red, green, and yellow balls, then sum all of three is equal to multiple of 45 by the square purple balls

How many balls of each color?

*) There are 81 balls, with four different colors, red, green, yellow, purple.

If square of the red, green, and yellow balls, then sum all of three is equal to multiple of 21 by the square purple balls

How many balls of each color?

*) There are 729 balls, with four different colors of red, green, yellow, and purple.

If the square of the red, green, and yellow balls, then sum all of three is equal to multiple of 30 by the square purple balls

How many balls of each color?

*) There are 345 balls, with four different colors, red, green, yellow, purple.

If square of the red, green, and yellow balls, then sum all of three is equal to multiple of 78 by the square purple balls

How many balls of each color?

*) There are 468 balls, with four different colors, red, green, yellow, purple.

If square of the red, green, and yellow balls, then sum all of three is equal to multiple of 227 by the square purple balls

How many balls of each color?

*) There are 368 balls, with four different colors, red, green, yellow, purple.

If square of the red, green, and yellow balls, then sum all of three is equal to multiple of 69 by the square purple balls

How many balls of each color?

*) There are 40 balls, with four different colors, red, green, yellow, purple.

If square of the red, green, and yellow balls, thn sum all of three is equal to multiple of 13 by the square purple balls

How many balls of each color?

*) There are many balls in box, with four different colors, red, green, yellow, and purple.

If the second power of red, green, and yellow balls, then sum all of three is equal to multiple of 29 by the square purple balls

Given: 25 purple balls
How many balls in the box more than?

How many balls of each color?

*) There are many balls in box, with four different colors, red, green, yellow, and purple.

If the second power of red, green, and yellow balls, then sum all of three is equal to multiple of 21 by the square purple balls

Given: 75 purple balls

How many balls in the box more than?

How many balls of each color?

*) There are many balls in box, with four different colors, red, green, yellow, and purple.

If the second power of red, green, and yellow balls, then sum all of three is equal to multiple of 51 by the square purple balls

Given: 30 purple balls

How many balls in the box more than?

How many balls of each color?

*) There are many balls in box, with four different colors, red, green, yellow, and purple.

If the second power of red, green, and yellow balls, then sum all of three is equal to multiple of 74 by the square purple balls

Given: 75 purple balls
How many balls in the box more than?
How many balls of each color?

*) There are many balls in box, with four different colors, red, green, yellow, and purple.
If the second power of red, green, and yellow balls, then sum all of three is equal to multiple of 145 by the square purple balls

Given: 215 purple balls
How many balls in the box more than?
How many balls of each color?

DIOPHANTINE EQUATION
Exponent 3

Diophantine equation with form

$$x^n + b \cdot y^n = z^n$$

There are many forms of the Diophantine equations and many other popular methods for each form, so I have shown a few forms for the Diophantine equations.

Example:

The Diophantine equation

$$x^n + b \cdot y^n = z^n$$

Another method, instead of the popular method above

The Diophantine eqution

$$a \cdot x^n + b \cdot y^n = c \cdot z^n$$

I synthesized between the popular method and Fermat's Last Theorem. We have a General method for the solution of the Diophantine equations above:

Other Diophantine eqution

$$a \cdot x^m + b \cdot y^n = c \cdot z^p$$
$$1/m + 1/n + 1/p < 1$$

Back to the Fermat-Wiles equation of the form with exponent 3 or greater than 3

$$x^n + y^n = c \cdot z^n \text{ with } n = 3$$
$$x^3 + y^3 = c \cdot z^3$$

The Diophantine equation $x^3 + y^3 = c \cdot z^3$ above, we find the values of c with n = 3, applying the popular method below

$$\zeta(s) = r^n + s^n = c$$

$$s = \sqrt[n]{c - r^n}$$
$$r = \sqrt[n]{c - s^n}$$

$$\zeta(s) = c \,\, \& \,\, \zeta(c) = 0$$

$$x = r \cdot z = \sqrt[n]{c - s^n} \cdot z$$
$$y = s \cdot z = \sqrt[n]{c - r^n} \cdot z$$

$$n \to \infty$$

THE VALUES OF C $n = 3$

$\zeta(s) = r^3 + s^3 = c$

$r^3 + s^3 = c$

$1^3 + 1^3 = 2$

$(37/21)^3 + (17/21)^3 = 6$

$2^3 + (-1)^3 = 7$

$1^3 + 2^3 = 9$

$2^3 + 2^3 = 16$

$3^3 + (-2)^3 = (5/2)^3 + (3/2)^3 = (15/10)^3 + (25/10)^3 = 19$

$3^3 + (-1)^3 = 26$

$1^3 + 3^3 = 28$

$3^3 + 2^3 = 35$

$4^3 + (-3)^3 = 37$

$(5/10)^3 + (35/10)^3 = (7/2)^3 + (1/2)^3 = 43$

$4^3 + (-2)^3 = 56$

$5^3 + (-4)^3 = 61$

$4^3 + (-1)^3 = 63$

$4^3 + 1^3 = 65$

$4^3 + 2^3 = 72$

$4^3 + 3^3 = 6^3 + (-5)^3 = 91$

$5^3 + (-3)^3 = 98$

$5^3 + (-2)^3 = 117$

$5^3 + (-1)^3 = 124$

$5^3 + 1^3 = 126$

$7^3 + (-6)^3 = 127$

$4^3 + 4^3 = 128$

$5^3 + 2^3 = 133$

$(35/10)^3 + (45/10)^3 = 134$

$5^3 + 3^3 = 6^3 + (-4)^3 = 152$

$8^3 + (-7)^3 = 169$

$(25/10)^3 + (55/10)^3 = 182$

$5^3 + 4^3 = 6^3 + (-3)^3 = 189$

$6^3 + (-2)^3 = 208$

$6^3 + (-1)^3 = 215$

$6^3 + 1^3 = 9^3 + (-8)^3 = 217$

$7^3 + (-5)^3 = 218$

$6^3 + 2^3 = 224$

$6^3 + 3^3 = 243$

$5^3 + 5^3 = 250$

$10^3 + (-9)^3 = 271$

$(65/10)^3 + (15/10)^3 = 278$

$7^3 + (-4^3) = 279$

$6^3 + 4^3 = 280$

$8^3 + (-6)^3 = 296$

$7^3 + (-3)^3 = 316$

$11^3 + (-10)^3 = 331$

$7^3 + (-2)^3 = 335$

$6^3 + 5^3 = 341$

$7^3 + (-1)^3 = 342$

$$7^3 + 1^3 = 344$$
$$7^3 + 2^3 = 351$$
$$7^3 + 3^3 = 370$$
$$9^3 + (-7^3) = 386$$
$$8^3 + (-5^3) = 387$$
$$12^3 + (-11)^3 = 397$$
$$7^3 + 4^3 = 407$$
$$6^3 + 6^3 = 432$$
$$8^3 + (-4)^3 = 448$$
$$7^3 + 5^3 = 468$$
$$13^3 + (-12)^3 = 469$$
$$10^3 + (-8)^3 = 488$$
$$8^3 + 1^3 = 513$$
$$8^3 + 2^3 = 520$$
$$83 + 33 = 539$$
$$143 + (-13)3 = 547$$
$$73 + 63 = 559$$

...

On internet we see

C-sequence for n = 3

For the sake of economy, let us list only the cube-free members of the c-sequence C corresponding to n = 3. The c-sequence is homogeneous in the sense that c is in C if and only if all cube-multiples of c are in C.

2, 6, 7, 9, 12, 13, 15, 17, 19, 20, 22, 26, 28, 30, 31, 33, 34, 35, 37, 42, 43, 49, 50, 51, 53, 58, 61, 62, 63, 65, 67, 68, 69, 70, 71, 75, 78, 79, 84, 85, 86, 87, 89, 90, 91, 92, 94, 97, 98, 103, 105, 106, 107, 110, 114, 115, 117, 123, 124, 126, 127, 130, 132, 133, 134, 139, 140, 141, 142, 143, 151, 153, 156, 157, 159, 161, 163, 164, 166, 169, 170, 171, 172, 177, 178, 179, 180, 182, 183, 186, 187, 193, 195, 197, 198, 201, 202, 203, 205, 206, 209, 210, 211, 212, 213, 214, 215, 217, 218, 219, 222, 223, 228, 229, 231, 233, 236, 238, 241, 244, 246, 247, 249, 251, 254, 258, 259, 265, 267, 269, 271, 273, 274, 275, 277, 278, 279, 282, 283, 284, 285, 286, 287, 289, 294, 295, 301, 303, 305, 306, 308, 309, 310, 313, 314, 316, 319, 321, 322, 323, 325, 330, 331, 333, 335, 337, 339, 341, 342, 345, 346, 348, 349, 355, 356, 357, 358, 359, 363, 366, 367, 370, 372, 373, 377, 379, 380, 382, 385, 386, 387, 388, 390, 391, 393, 394, 395, 396, 397, 399, 402, 403, 407, 409, 411, 413, 414, 418, 420, 421, 422, 425, 427, 428, 429, 430, 431, 433, 435, 436, 438, 439, 441, 444, 445, 446, 447, 449, 450, 452, 453, 454, 457, 458, 460, 462, 463, 465, 466, 467, 468, 469, 474, 477, 481, 483, 484, 485, 490, 493, 494, 495, 497, 498, 499, ..."

APPLICATIONS

*) Find the values of x, y, z, of the Fermat-Wiles equation following

$$x^3 + y^3 = 19 \cdot z^3$$

(x, y, z must get integers)

Solve

The Diophantine equation

$$x^3 + y^3 = 19 \cdot z^3$$

Find the values of c

Applying the popular method

$$\zeta(s) = r^n + s^n = c$$

$$s = \sqrt[n]{c - r^n}$$

$$r = \sqrt[n]{c - s^n}$$

$$\zeta(s) = c \ \& \ \zeta(c) = 0$$

$$x = r \cdot z = \sqrt[n]{c - s^n} \cdot z$$

$$y = s \cdot z = \sqrt[n]{c - r^n} \cdot z$$

$$n \rightarrow \infty$$

Or

$$r^3 + s^3 = c = 19$$

Find the values of r and s

$$c = 19$$
$$\zeta(s) = r^3 + s^3 = 19$$
$$\zeta(s)_1 = 3^3 + (-2)^3 = 19$$
$$\zeta(s)_2 = (5/2)^3 + (3/2)^3 = 19$$
$$\zeta(s)_3 = (15/10)^3 + (25/10)^3 = 19$$

The first approach to

$$\zeta(s)_1 = 3^3 + (-2)^3 = 19$$

And we get

$$x = r \cdot z$$
$$y = s \cdot z$$

The value of z

Choose any value of z (i.e., 1, 2, 3, 4, …)

$$z = 4$$

The value of x

$$x = r \cdot z$$
$$x = 3 \cdot 4 = 12$$

The value of y

$$y = s \cdot z$$
$$y = -2 \cdot 4 = -8$$

Try again

Replace these values into equation

$$x^3 + y^3 = 19 \cdot z^3$$

$$12^3 - 8^3 = 19 \cdot 4^3 = 1216$$

Solution 1: x = 12, y = -8, z = 4

The second approach to

$$\zeta(s)_2 = (5/2)^3 + (3/2)^3 = 19$$

And we get

$$x = r \cdot z$$

$$y = s \cdot z$$

The value of z

Choose the value of z ≡ mod 2 (i.e., 2, 4, 6, 8...)

$$z = 6$$

The value of x

$$x = r \cdot z$$

$$x = 5/2 \cdot 6 = 15$$

The value of y

$$y = s \cdot z$$

$$y = 3/2 \cdot 6 = 9$$

Try again

Replace these values into the equation

$$x^3 + y^3 = 19 \cdot z^3$$

$$15^3 + 9^3 = 19 \cdot 6^3 = 4104$$

Solution 2: x = 15, y = 9, z = 6

The third approach to

$$\zeta(s)_3 = (15/10)^3 + (25/10)^3 = 19$$

And we get

$$x = r \cdot z$$
$$y = s \cdot z$$

The value of z

Choose the value of $z \equiv$ mod 10 (i.e., 10, 20, 30, 40...)

$$z = 20$$

The value of x

$$x = r \cdot z$$
$$x = 15/10 \cdot 20 = 30$$

The value of y

$$y = s \cdot z$$
$$y = 25/10 \cdot 20 = 50$$

Try again

Replace these values

$$x^3 + y^3 = 19 \cdot z^3$$
$$30^3 + 50^3 = 19 \cdot 20^3 = 152000$$

Solution 3: x = 30, y = 50, z = 20

Solution:

$$x = 12, y = -8, z = 4$$
$$x = 15, y = 9, z = 6$$
$$x = 30, y = 50, z = 20$$

*) Find the values of x, y, z which whole numbers of the Fermat- Wiles Equation below

$$x^3 + y^3 = 43 \cdot z^3$$

Solve

Fermat- Wiles Equation:

$$x^3 + y^3 = 43 \cdot z^3$$

Applying the popular method

$$\zeta(s) = r^n + s^n = c$$

$$s = \sqrt[n]{c - r^n}$$
$$r = \sqrt[n]{c - s^n}$$
$$\zeta(s) = c \ \& \ \zeta(c) = 0$$
$$x = r \cdot z = \sqrt[n]{c - s^n} \cdot z$$
$$y = s \cdot z = \sqrt[n]{c - r^n} \cdot z$$

$$n \to \infty$$

Find the values of r, s

$$c = 43$$
$$\zeta(s) = r^3 + s^3 = 43$$
$$\zeta(s)_1 = (5/10)^3 + (35/10)^3 = 43$$
$$\zeta(s)_2 = (7/2)^3 + (1/2)^3 = 43$$

The first approach to

$$\zeta(s)_1 = (5/10)^3 + (35/10)^3 = 43$$

And we have

$$x = r \cdot z$$
$$y = s \cdot z$$

The value of z

Choose the value of z must mod 10 (i.e., 10, 20, 30, 40, …)

$$z = 30$$

The value of x

$$x = r \cdot z$$
$$x = 5/10 \cdot 30 = 15$$

The value of y

$$y = s \cdot z$$
$$y = 35/10 \cdot 30 = 105$$

Replace these values to try again

$$x^3 + y^3 = 43 \cdot z^3$$
$$15^3 + 105^3 = 43 \cdot 30^3 = 1161000$$

Solution 1: x = 15, y = 105, z = 30

The second approach to

$$\zeta(s)_2 = (7/2)^3 + (1/2)^3 = 43$$

And we have

$$x = r \cdot z$$
$$y = s \cdot z$$

The value of z

Choose the value of z must mod 2 (i.e., 2, 4, 6, 8...)

$$z = 2$$

The value of x

$$x = r \cdot z$$
$$x = 7/2 \cdot 2 = 7$$

The value of y

$$y = s \cdot z$$
$$y = 1/2 \cdot 2 = 1$$

Replace these values to try again

$$x^3 + y^3 = 43 \cdot z^3$$
$$7^3 + 1^3 = 43 \cdot 2^3 = 344$$

Solution 2: x = 7, y = 1, z = 2

Solution:

$$x = 15, y = 105, z = 30$$
$$x = 7, y = 1, z = 2$$

---

*) Find the values of x, y, z which whole numbers of the Fermat- Wiles Equation below

$$x^3 + y^3 = 370 \cdot z^3$$

Given: x + y + z = 121

Solve

Fermat- Wiles Equation:

$$x^3 + y^3 = 370 \cdot z^3$$

Applying the popular method

$$\zeta(s) = r^n + s^n = c$$

$$s = \sqrt{c - r}$$
$$r = \sqrt[n]{c - s^n}$$
$$\zeta(s) = c \ \& \ \zeta(c) = 0$$
$$x = r \cdot z = \sqrt[n]{c - s^n \cdot z}$$
$$y = s \cdot z = \sqrt[n]{c - r^n \cdot z}$$

$$n \to \infty$$

Find the values of r, s

$$c = 370$$
$$\zeta(s) = r^3 + s^3 = 370$$
$$\zeta(s)_1 = 7^3 + 3^3 = 370$$

The value of z

We have

$$x + y + z = 121$$

And r + s = 7 + 3 = 10

Then

$$z = \frac{121}{r+s+1} = \frac{121}{11} = 11$$

The value of x

$$x = r \cdot z$$
$$x = 7 \cdot 11 = 77$$

The value of y

$$y = s \cdot z$$
$$y = 3 \cdot 11 = 33$$

Try again

Replace these values

$$x + y + z = 121$$
$$77 + 33 + 11 = 121$$

And

$$x^3 + y^3 = 370 \cdot z^3$$
$$77^3 + 33^3 = 370 \cdot 11^3$$
$$456533 + 35937 = 492470$$

Solution

$$x = 77, \; y = 33, \; z = 11$$

———————————————

*) Find the values of x, y, z which whole numbers of the Fermat- Wiles Equation below

$$x^3 + y^3 = 637 \cdot z^3$$

Given: $x + y + z = 98$

Solve

Fermat- Wiles Equation:

$$x^3 + y^3 = 637 \cdot z^3$$

Applying the popular method

$$\zeta(s) = r^n + s^n = c$$

$$s = \sqrt[n]{c - r^n}$$
$$r = \sqrt[n]{c - s^n}$$
$$\zeta(s) = c \;\&\; \zeta(c) = 0$$
$$x = r \cdot z = \sqrt[n]{c - s^n \cdot z}$$
$$y = s \cdot z = \sqrt[n]{c - r^n \cdot z}$$

$$n \to \infty$$

Find the values of r, s

$$c = 637$$
$$\zeta(s) = r^3 + s^3 = 637$$
$$\zeta(s)_1 = 5^3 + 8^3 = 637$$

116

The value of z

We have

$$x + y + z = 98$$

And $r + s = 5 + 8 = 13$

Then

$$z = \frac{98}{r + s + 1} = \frac{98}{14} = 7$$

The value of x

$$x = r \cdot z$$
$$x = 5 \cdot 7 = 35$$

The value of y

$$y = s \cdot z$$
$$y = 8 \cdot 7 = 56$$

Replace these values to try again

$$x + y + z = 98$$
$$35 + 56 + 7 = 98$$

And $x^3 + y^3 = 637 \cdot z^3$

$$35^3 + 56^3 = 637 \cdot 7^3$$
$$= 218491$$

Solution

$$x = 35, \ y = 56, \ z = 7$$

*) Find the values of x, y, z which whole numbers of the Fermat- Wiles Equation below:

$$x^3 + y^3 = 217 \cdot z^3$$

Given: $x + y + z = 56$

Solve

Fermat- Wiles Equation:

$$x^3 + y^3 = 217 \cdot z^3$$

Applying the popular method

$$\zeta(s) = r^n + s^n = c$$

$$s = \sqrt[n]{c - r^n}$$
$$r = \sqrt[n]{c - s^n}$$
$$\zeta(s) = c \ \& \ \zeta(c) = 0$$
$$x = r \cdot z = \sqrt[n]{c - s^n \cdot z}$$
$$y = s \cdot z = \sqrt[n]{c - r^n \cdot z}$$

$$n \rightarrow \infty$$

Find the values of r, s

$$c = 217$$
$$\zeta(s) = r^3 + s^3 = 217$$
$$\zeta(s)_1 = 6^3 + 1^3 = 217$$
$$\zeta(s)_2 = 9^3 + (-8)^3 = 217$$

The first approach to

$$\zeta(s)_1 = 6^3 + 1^3 = 217$$

And

$$x = r \cdot z$$
$$y = s \cdot z$$

The value of z

We have

$$x + y + z = 56$$

And $r + s = 6 + 1 = 7$

Then

$$z = \frac{56}{r + s + 1} = \frac{56}{8} = 7$$

The value of x

$$x = r \cdot z$$
$$x = 6 \cdot 7 = 42$$

The value of y

$$y = s \cdot z$$
$$y = 1 \cdot 7 = 7$$

Replace these values to try again

$$x + y + z = 56$$
$$42 + 7 + 7 = 56$$

And $x^3 + y^3 = 217 \cdot z^3$

$$42^3 + 7^3 = 217 \cdot 7^3$$
$$= 74431$$

Solution 1: x = 42, y = 7, z = 7

The second approach to

$$\zeta(s)_2 = 9^3 + (-8)^3 = 217$$

$$x = r \cdot z$$
$$y = s \cdot z$$

The value of z

We have

$$x + y + z = 56$$

And r + s = 9 + (-8) = 1

Then

$$z = \frac{56}{r+s+1} = \frac{56}{2} = 28$$

The value of x

$$x = r \cdot z$$
$$x = 9 \cdot 28 = 252$$

The value of y

$$y = s \cdot z$$
$$y = -8 \cdot 28 = -224$$

Replace these values to try again

$$x + y + z = 56$$
$$252 + (-224) + 28 = 56$$

And

$$x^3 + y^3 = 217 \cdot z^3$$
$$252^3 + (-224)^3 = 217 \cdot 28^3$$
$$= 4763584$$

Solution: $x = 42$, $y = 7$, $z = 7$

$$x = 252, \ y = -224, \ z = 28$$

---

*) Find the values of x, y, and z, which whole numbers of the Fermat- Wiles Equation below:

$$x^3 + y^3 = 189 \cdot z^3$$
Given: $x + y + z = 20$

Solve

Fermat- Wiles Equation:

$$x^3 + y^3 = 189 \cdot z^3$$

Applying the popular method:

$$\zeta(s) = r^n + s^n = c$$

$$s = \sqrt[n]{c - r^n}$$
$$r = \sqrt[n]{c - s^n}$$
$$\zeta(s) = c \ \& \ \zeta(c) = 0$$
$$x = r \cdot z = \sqrt[n]{c - s^n \cdot z}$$
$$y = s \cdot z = \sqrt[n]{c - r^n \cdot z}$$

$$n \to \infty$$

Find the values of r, s

$$c = 189$$
$$\zeta(s) = r^3 + s^3 = 189$$
$$\zeta(s)_1 = 5^3 + 4^3 = 189$$
$$\zeta(s)_2 = 6^3 + (-3)^3 = 189$$

The first approach to

$$\zeta(s)_1 = 5^3 + 4^3 = 189$$

$$x = r \cdot z$$
$$y = s \cdot z$$

The value of z

We have

$$x + y + z = 20$$

And r + s = 5 + 4 = 9

Then

$$z = \frac{20}{r+s+1} = \frac{20}{10} = 2$$

The value of x

$$x = r \cdot z$$
$$x = 5 \cdot 2 = 10$$

The value of y

$$y = s \cdot z$$
$$y = 4 \cdot 2 = 8$$

Replace these values to try again

$$x + y + z = 20$$
$$10 + 8 + 2 = 20$$

And

$$x^3 + y^3 = 189 \cdot z^3$$
$$10^3 + 8^3 = 189 \cdot 2^3$$
$$= 1512$$

Solution 1: x = 10, y = 8, z = 2

The second approach to

$$\zeta(s)_2 = 6^3 + (-3)^3 = 189$$
$$x = r \cdot z$$
$$y = s \cdot z$$

The value of z

We have

$$x + y + z = 20$$

And $r + s = 6 + (-3) = 3$

Then

$$z = \frac{20}{r+s+1} = \frac{20}{4} = 5$$

The value of x

$$x = r \cdot z$$
$$x = 6 \cdot 5 = 30$$

The value of y

$$y = s \cdot z$$
$$y = -3 \cdot 5 = -15$$

Replace these values to try again

$$x + y + z = 20$$
$$30 + (-15) + 5 = 20$$

And $x^3 + y^3 = 189 \cdot z^3$

$$30^3 + (-15)^3 = 189 \cdot 5^3$$
$$= 23625$$

Solution: x = 10, y = 8, z = 2

x = 30, y = -15, z = 5

*) There are many balls in the box, with three different colors, green, yellow, and purple. If the 3rd power of the green, and yellow balls, sum of both, it's equal to multiple of 91 by the third powers of purple balls

Given: 17 purple balls

How many balls in the box more than?

How many balls of each color?

Solve

We put

A = green balls

B = yellow balls

C = purple balls

We have

$$F_1(s) = A^3 + B^3 = 91 \cdot C^3$$

Back to Fermat Wiles equaion

$$x^n + y^n = c \cdot z^n$$

Applying the popular method, with $n = 3$

$$\zeta(s) = r^n + s^n = c$$

$$s = \sqrt[n]{c - r^n}$$

$$r = \sqrt[n]{c - s^n}$$
$$\zeta(s) = c \ \& \ \zeta(c) = 0$$
$$x = r \cdot z = \sqrt[n]{c - s^n \cdot z}$$
$$y = s \cdot z = \sqrt[n]{c - r^n \cdot z}$$
$$n \to \infty$$

The values of A, B, C

$$\zeta(s) = c \text{ and } \zeta(c) = 0$$

Find the values of r, s

$$c = 91$$
$$\zeta(s) = r^3 + s^3 = 91$$
$$\zeta(s)_1 = 3^3 + 4^3 = 91$$
$$\zeta(s)_2 = 6^3 + (-5)^3 = 91$$

The first approach to

$$\zeta(s) = 3^3 + 4^3 = 91$$

$$A = 3 \cdot C$$
$$B = 4 \cdot C$$

The values of A, B

$$C = 17 \text{ balls}$$
$$A = 3 \cdot C = 3 \cdot 17 = 51 \text{ balls}$$
$$B = 4 \cdot C = 4 \cdot 17 = 68 \text{ balls}$$

Replace these values into F1 (s) to try again

$$F_1(s) = A^3 + B^3 = 91 \cdot C^3$$
$$= 51^3 + 68^3 = 91 \cdot 17^3 = 447083$$

Solution 1:

A = green balls: 51

B = yellow balls 68

C = purple balls 17

A + B + C

51 + 68 + 17 = 136 Balls

The second approach to

$$\zeta(s) = 6^3 + (-5^3) = 91$$
$$A = 6 \cdot C$$
$$B = -5 \cdot C$$

The values of A, B

C = 17 balls

$A = 6 \cdot C = 6 \cdot 17 = 102$ balls

$B = -5 \cdot C = -5 \cdot 17 = -85$ balls (we do not get)

Solution:

A = green balls: 51

B = yellow balls 68

C = purple balls 17

51 + 68 + 17 = 136 Balls

….

~~~~~~~//////~~~~~~~

*) There are many balls in box, with three different colors, green, yellow, purple, if the third powers of the green, and yellow balls, then sum of both, it's equal to the 4th power of purple balls

Given: 152 purple balls
How many balls in the box more than?
How many balls of each color?

Solve

We put

A= green balls
B = yellow balls
C = purple balls

We have
$$F_1(s) = A^3 + B^3 = C^4$$

Rewrite the Diophantine equation $F_1(s)$
$$F_1(s) = A^3 + B^3 = C \cdot C^3$$

Back to problem Fermat -Wiles equaion

$$x^n + y^n = c \cdot z^n$$

Applying the popular method, n = 3

$$\zeta(s) = r^n + s^n = c$$

$$s = \sqrt[n]{c - r^n}$$

$$r = \sqrt[n]{c - s^n}$$

$$\zeta(s) = c \ \& \ \zeta(c) = 0$$

$$x = r \cdot z = \sqrt[n]{c - s^n} \cdot z$$

$$y = s \cdot z = \sqrt[n]{c - r^n} \cdot z$$

$$n \to \infty$$

The values of A, B, C

$$\zeta(s) = c \text{ and } \zeta(c) = 0$$

Find the values of r, s

$$c = C = 152$$

$$\zeta(s) = r^3 + s^3 = 152$$

$$\zeta(s)_1 = 5^3 + 3^3 = 152$$

$$\zeta(s)_2 = 6^3 + (-4)^3 = 152$$

The first approach to

$$\zeta(s) = 5^3 + 3^3 = 152$$

$$A = 5 \cdot C$$

$$B = 3 \cdot C$$

The values of A, B

$$C = 152 \text{ balls}$$
$$A = 5 \cdot C = 5 \cdot 152 = 760 \text{ balls}$$
$$B = 3 \cdot C = 3 \cdot 152 = 456 \text{ balls}$$

Replace these values in $F_1(s)$ to try again

$$F_1(s) = A^3 + B^3 = C^4$$
$$= 760^3 + 456^3 = 152^4 = 533794816$$

Solution 1:

A = green balls: 760

B = yellow balls 456

C = purple balls 152

A + B + C

760 + 456 + 152 = 1368 Balls

The second approach to

$$\zeta(s)_2 = 6^3 + (-4)^3 = 152$$
$$A = 6 \cdot C$$
$$B = -4 \cdot C$$

The values of A, B

C = 152 balls

$A = 6 \cdot C = 6 \cdot 152 = 912$ balls

$B = -4 \cdot C = -4 \cdot 152 = -608$ balls (we do not get)

Solution

A = green balls: 760

B = yellow balls 456

C = purple balls 152

760 + 456 + 152 = 1368 Balls

…

~~~~~~~//////~~~~~~

*) There are many balls in box, with three different colors, green, yellow, purple, if the third powers of the green, and yellow balls, then sum of both, it's equal to the 4th power of purple balls

Given: 217 purple balls

How many balls in the box more than?

How many balls of each color?

Solve

We put

A= green balls

B = yellow balls

C = purple balls

We have

$$F_1(s) = A^3 + B^3 = C^4$$

Rewrite the Diophantine equation $F_1(s)$

$$F_1(s) = A^3 + B^3 = C \cdot C^3$$

Back to problem Fermat -Wiles equaion

$$x^n + y^n = c \cdot z^n$$

Applying the popular method, $n = 3$

$$\zeta(s) = r^n + s^n = c$$

$$s = \sqrt[n]{c - r^n}$$
$$r = \sqrt[n]{c - s^n}$$
$$\zeta(s) = c \; \& \; \zeta(c) = 0$$
$$x = r \cdot z = \sqrt[n]{c - s^n \cdot z}$$
$$y = s \cdot z = \sqrt[n]{c - r^n \cdot z}$$

$$n \to \infty$$

The values of A, B, C

$$\zeta(s) = c \text{ and } \zeta(c) = 0$$

Find the values of r, s

$$c = C = 217$$
$$\zeta(s) = r^3 + s^3 = 217$$
$$\zeta(s)_1 = 6^3 + 1^3 = 217$$
$$\zeta(s)_2 = 9^3 + (-8)^3 = 217$$

The first approach to

$$\zeta(s) = 6^3 + 1^3 = 217$$

$$A = 6 \cdot C$$
$$B = 1 \cdot C$$

The values of A, B

C = 217 balls
$$A = 6 \cdot C = 6 \cdot 217 = 1302 \text{ balls}$$
$$B = 1 \cdot C = 1 \cdot 217 = 217 \text{ balls}$$

Replace these values in $F_1(s)$ to try again

$$F_1(s) = A^3 + B^3 = C^4$$
$$= 1302^3 + 217^3 = 217^4 = 2217373921$$

Solution 1:

A = green balls: 1302
B = yellow balls 217
C = purple balls 217
A + B + C
1302 + 217 + 217 = 1736 Balls

The second approach to

$$\zeta(s)_2 = 9^3 + (-8)^3 = 217$$
$$A = 9 \cdot C$$
$$B = -8 \cdot C$$

The values of A, B

C = 217 balls

A = 9 · C = 9 · 217 = 1953 balls

B = -8 · C = -8 · 217 = -1736 balls

(not get)

Solution:

A = green balls: 1302

B = yellow balls 217

C = purple balls 217

1302 + 217 + 217 = 1736 Balls

———————————

EXERCISES

*) Find the values of x, y, z, of the Fermat-Wiles equation following

All the unknowns take integer values

$$x^3 + y^3 = 6 \cdot z^3$$

*) Find the values of x, y, z, of the Fermat-Wiles equation following

All the unknowns take integer values

$$x^3 + y^3 = 7 \cdot z^3$$

*) Find the values of x, y, z, of the Fermat-Wiles equation following

All the unknowns take integer values

$$x^3 + y^3 = 35 \cdot z^3$$

*) Find the values of x, y, z, of the Fermat-Wiles equation following

All the unknowns take integer values
$$x^3 + y^3 = 37 \cdot z^3$$

*) Find the values of x, y, z, of the Fermat-Wiles equation following
All the unknowns take integer values
$$x^3 + y^3 = 61 \cdot z^3$$

*) Find the values of x, y, z, of the Fermat-Wiles equation following
All the unknowns take integer values
$$x^3 + y^3 = 72 \cdot z^3$$

*) Find the values of x, y, z, of the Fermat-Wiles equation following
All the unknowns take integer values
$$x^3 + y^3 = 98 \cdot z^3$$

*) Find the values of x, y, z, of the Fermat-Wiles equation following
All the unknowns take integer values
$$x^3 + y^3 = 117 \cdot z^3$$

*) Find the values of x, y, z, of the Fermat-Wiles equation following

All the unknowns take integer values

$$x^3 + y^3 = 127 \cdot z^3$$

*) Find the values of x, y, z, of the Fermat-Wiles equation following

All the unknowns take integer values

$$x^3 + y^3 = 133 \cdot z^3$$

*) Find the values of x, y, z, of the Fermat-Wiles equation following

All the unknowns take integer values

$$x^3 + y^3 = 134 \cdot z^3$$

*) Find the values of x, y, z, of the Fermat-Wiles equation following

All the unknowns take integer values

$$x^3 + y^3 = 182 \cdot z^3$$

*) Find the values of x, y, z, of the Fermat-Wiles equation following

All the unknowns take integer values

$$x^3 + y^3 = 224 \cdot z^3$$

*) Find the values of x, y, z, of the Fermat-Wiles equation following

All the unknowns take integer values

$$x^3 + y^3 = 279 \cdot z^3$$

*) Find the values of x, y, z, of the Fermat-Wiles equation following

All the unknowns take integer values

$$x^3 + y^3 = 280 \cdot z^3$$

*) Find the values of x, y, z, of the Fermat-Wiles equation following

All the unknowns take integer values

$$x^3 + y^3 = 296 \cdot z^3$$

*) Find the values of x, y, z, of the Fermat-Wiles equation following

All the unknowns take integer values

$$x^3 + y^3 = 316 \cdot z^3$$

*) Find the values of x, y, z, of the Fermat-Wiles equation following

All the unknowns take integer values

$$x^3 + y^3 = 331 \cdot z^3$$

*) There are many balls in box, with three different colors, green, yellow, purple, if the third power of the green, and yellow balls, then sum of both, it's equal to multiply of 344 by the third power of purple balls

Given: 13 purple balls
How many balls of each color?

*) There are many balls in box, with three different colors, green, yellow, purple, if the third power of the green, and yellow balls, then sum of both, it's equal to multiple of 351 by the third power of purple balls

Given: 23 purple balls
How many balls of each color?

*) There are many balls in box, with three different colors, green, yellow, purple, if the third power of the green, and yellow balls, then sum of both, it's equal to multiple of 407 by the third power of purple balls

Given: 31 purple balls
How many balls of each color?

*) There are many balls in box, with three different colors, green, yellow, purple, if the third power of the green, and yellow balls, thn sum of both, it's equal to multiple of 432 by the third power of purple balls

Given: 19 purple balls
How many balls of each color?

*) There are many balls in box, with three different colors, green, yellow, purple, if the third power of the green, and yellow balls, then sum of both, it's equal to multiple of 468 by the third power of purple balls

Given: 39 purple balls
How many balls of each color?

*) There are many balls in box, with three different colors, green, yellow, purple, if the third power of the green, and yellow balls, then sum of both, it's equal to multiple of 513 by the third power of purple balls

Given: 13 purple balls
How many balls of each color?

*) There are many balls in box, with three different colors, green, yellow, purple, if the third power of the green, and yellow balls, then sum of both, it's equal to multiple of 520 by the third power of purple balls

Given: 37 purple balls
How many balls of each color?

*) There are many balls in box, with three different colors, green, yellow, purple, if the third power of the green, and yellow balls, then sum of both, it's equal to multiple of 539 by the third power of purple balls

Given: 42 purple balls
How many balls of each color?

*) There are many balls in box, with three different colors, green, yellow, purple, if the third power of the green, and yellow balls, then sum of both, it's equal to multiple of 559 by the third power of purple balls

Given: 47 purple balls
How many balls of each color?

*) There are many balls in box, with three different colors, green, yellow, purple, if the third power of the green, and yellow balls, then sum of both, it's equal to the 4th power of purple balls

Given: 1008 purple balls
How many balls of each color?

*) There are many balls in box, with three different colors, green, yellow, purple, if the third power of the green, and yellow balls, then sum of both, it's equal to the 4th power of purple balls

Given: 1027 purple balls
How many balls of each color?

*) There are many balls in box, with three different colors, green, yellow, purple, if the third power of the green, and yellow balls, then sum of both, it's equal to the 4th power of purple balls

Given: 1339 purple balls
How many balls of each color?

*) There are many balls in box, with three different colors, green, yellow, purple, if the third power of the green, and yellow balls, then sum of both, it's equal to the 4th power of purple balls

Given: 1358 purple balls
How many balls of each color?

*) There are many balls in box, with three different colors, green, yellow, purple, if the third power of the green, and yellow balls, then sum of both, it's equal to the 4th power of purple balls

Given: 1456 purple balls
How many balls of each color?

*) There are many balls in box, with three different colors, green, yellow, purple, if the third power of the green, and yellow balls, then sum of both, it's equal to the 4th power of purple balls

Given: 1729 purple balls
How many balls of each color?

EXPAND DIOPHANTINE EQUATIONS
$v^n + x^n + y^n = z^n$

On internet we see:

"R. E. Frye, Finding $95800^4 + 217519^4 + 414560^4 = 422481^4$ on the Connection Machine (1988)"

We can use the popular method, for solution of the Diophantine Equation, which takes form

$$v^n + x^n + y^n = z^n$$

Applying the popular method, for the Generalized Fermat-Wiles Equation

$$\zeta(s) = r^n + s^n = c$$

$$s = \sqrt[n]{c - r^n}$$
$$r = \sqrt[n]{c - s^n}$$
$$\zeta(s) = c \ \& \ \zeta(c) = 0$$
$$x = r \cdot z = \sqrt[n]{c - s^n} \cdot z$$
$$y = s \cdot z = \sqrt[n]{c - r^n} \cdot z$$

$$n \to \infty$$

First we find the values of zeta function $\zeta(s)_1$ and the zeta function $\zeta(s)_2$, both zeta function $\zeta(s)$ is equal to c, also both the zeta function $\zeta(c)$ is equal to 0.

$$\zeta(s) = c \ \& \ \zeta(c) = 0$$

Example:

Diophantine equation:

$$v^2 + x^2 + y^2 = z^2$$

$$\zeta(s)_1 = r_1^2 + s_1^2 = c$$
$$\zeta(s)_2 = r_2^2 + s_2^2 = c$$

We have:

$$\zeta(s)_1 = r_1^2 + s_1^2 = 5^2 + 5^2 = 50$$
$$\zeta(s)_2 = r_2^2 + s_2^2 = 7^2 + 1^2 = 50$$

$$\zeta(s)_1 = r_1^2 + s_1^2 = 7^2 + 4^2 = 65$$
$$\zeta(s)_2 = r_2^2 + s_2^2 = 8^2 + 1^2 = 65$$

$$\zeta(s)_1 = r_1^2 + s_1^2 = 9^2 + 2^2 = 85$$
$$\zeta(s)_2 = r_2^2 + s_2^2 = 7^2 + 6^2 = 85$$

…..

Diophantine equation:

$$v^3 + x^3 + y^3 = z^3$$
$$\zeta(s)_1 = r_1^3 + s_1^3 = c$$
$$\zeta(s)_2 = r_2^3 + s_2^3 = c$$

and

$$\zeta(s)_1 = \zeta(s)_2 = c$$

$$\zeta(s)_1 = r_1{}^3 + s_1{}^3 = 6^3 + (-5)^3 = 91$$
$$\zeta(s)_2 = r_2{}^3 + s_2{}^3 = 3^3 + 4^3 = 91$$

$$\zeta(s)_1 = r_1{}^3 + s_1{}^3 = 6^3 + (-4)^3 = 152$$
$$\zeta(s)_2 = r_2{}^3 + s_2{}^3 = 3^3 + 5^3 = 152$$

$$\zeta(s)_1 = r_1{}^3 + s_1{}^3 = 6^3 + (-3)^3 = 189$$
$$\zeta(s)_2 = r_2{}^3 + s_2{}^3 = 5^3 + 4^3 = 189$$

$$\zeta(s)_1 = r_1{}^3 + s_1{}^3 = 9^3 + (-8)^3 = 217$$
$$\zeta(s)_2 = r_2{}^3 + s_2{}^3 = 6^3 + 1^3 = 217$$

$$\zeta(s)_1 = r_1{}^3 + s_1{}^3 = 9^3 + (-6)^3 = 513$$
$$\zeta(s)_2 = r_2{}^3 + s_2{}^3 = (9/2)^3 + (15/2)^3 = 513$$

$$\zeta(s)_1 = r_1{}^3 + s_1{}^3 = 12^3 + 1^3 = 1729$$
$$\zeta(s)_2 = r_2{}^3 + s_2{}^3 = 10^3 + 9^3 = 1729$$

...

Expanded from 3 unknowns of Fermat-Wiles equation to many unknowns

Example:

*) Find the values of a, b, c, d of the Diophantine equation below

$$a^3 + b^3 + c^3 = d^3$$

Unknowns take the whole numbers

Given: the smallest value has 2 digits

Solve

Used the popular method to find the values of a, b, c, d, …
as following

$$\zeta(s) = r^n + s^n = c$$

$$s = \sqrt[n]{c - r^n}$$
$$r = \sqrt[n]{c - s^n}$$
$$\zeta(s) = c \ \& \ \zeta(c) = 0$$
$$x = r \cdot z = \sqrt[n]{c - s^n \cdot z}$$
$$y = s \cdot z = \sqrt[n]{c - r^n \cdot z}$$
$$n \to \infty$$

There are many values of r and s as following

$$\zeta_1(s) = r^n + s^n = c$$

$$\zeta_1(s) = r^3 + s^3 = 91$$
$$4^3 + 3^3 = 91$$

147

And

$$\zeta_2(s) = r^n + s^n = c$$
$$\zeta_2(s) = r^3 + s^3 = 91$$
$$6^3 + (-5)^3 = 91$$

Other values of r, s

$$\zeta_1(s) = r^n + s^n = c$$

$$\zeta_1(s) = r^3 + s^3 = 189$$
$$5^3 + 4^3 = 189$$

And

$$\zeta_2(s) = r^n + s^n = c$$

$$\zeta_2(s) = r^3 + s^3 = 189$$
$$6^3 + (-3)^3 = 189$$

Other values of r, s

$$\zeta_1(s) = r^n + s^n = c$$

$$\zeta_1(s) = r^3 + s^3 = 217$$
$$6^3 + 1^3 = 217$$

And

$$\zeta_2(s) = r^n + s^n = c$$

$$\zeta_2(s) = r^3 + s^3 = 217$$
$$9^3 + (-8)^3 = 217$$

Next step

We use the popular method for finding the values of a, b, c, and d

$$\zeta(s) = r^n + s^n = c$$

$$s = \sqrt[n]{c - r^n}$$
$$r = \sqrt[n]{c - s^n}$$
$$\zeta(s) = c \ \& \ \zeta(c) = 0$$
$$x = r \cdot z = \sqrt[n]{c - s^n} \cdot z$$
$$y = s \cdot z = \sqrt[n]{c - r^n} \cdot z$$

$$n \to \infty$$

Back to the Fermat-Wiles Equation below

$$x^3 + y^3 = 91 \cdot z^3$$

The values of x, y, z

$$\zeta(s) = c \text{ and } \zeta(c) = 0$$

Find the values of r, s

$$c = 91$$
$$\zeta(s) = r^3 + s^3 = 91$$
$$\zeta(s)_1 = 4^3 + 3^3 = 91$$
$$\zeta(s)_2 = 6^3 + (-5)^3 = 91$$

The first approach to

$$\zeta(s) = 3^3 + 4^3 = 91$$
$$x = 3 \cdot z$$
$$y = 4 \cdot z$$

149

The values of x, y

Choose any value of z (z = 17)

$$x = 3 \cdot z = 3 \cdot 17 = 51$$
$$y = 4 \cdot z = 4 \cdot 17 = 68$$

Replace these values into $F_1(s)$

Try again

$$F_1(s) = x^3 + y^3 = 91 \cdot z^3$$
$$= 51^3 + 68^3 = 91 \cdot 17^3 = 447083$$

Solution 1:

$$x = 51, y = 68, z = 17$$

The second approach to

$$\zeta(s)_2 = 6^3 + (-5)^3 = 91$$
$$x = 6 \cdot z$$
$$y = -5 \cdot z$$

The values of x, y

$$z = 17$$
$$x = 6 \cdot z = 6 \cdot 17 = 102$$
$$y = -5 \cdot z = -5 \cdot 17 = -85$$

Replace these values into $F_2(s)$

Try again

$$F_2(s) = x^3 + y^3 = 91 \cdot z^3$$
$$= 102^3 + (-85)^3 = 91 \cdot 17^3 = 447083$$

Solution 2:

$$x = 102, y = -85, z = 17$$

From $F_1(s)$ and $F_2(s)$ we have

$$51^3 + 68^3 = 102^3 + (-85)^3 = 91 \cdot 17^3$$
$$= 447083$$

Or $51^3 + 68^3 = 102^3 + (-85)^3$

Then

$$51^3 + 68^3 + 85^3 = 102^3$$

Back to the Fermat-Wiles Equation below

$$x^3 + y^3 = 189 \cdot z^3$$
$$\zeta(s) = c \text{ and } \zeta(c) = 0$$

Find the values of r, s

$$r^3 + s^3 = 189$$
$$c = 189$$
$$\zeta(s) = r^3 + s^3 = 189$$
$$\zeta(s)_1 = 4^3 + 5^3 = 189$$
$$\zeta(s)_2 = 6^3 + (-3)^3 = 189$$

The first approach to

$$\zeta(s) = 4^3 + 5^3 = 189$$

$$x = 4 \cdot z$$
$$y = 5 \cdot z$$

The values of x, y

Choose any value of z (z = 37)

$$x = 4 \cdot z = 4 \cdot 37 = 148$$
$$y = 5 \cdot z = 5 \cdot 37 = 185$$

Replace these values into $F_1(s)$

Try again

$$F_1(s) = x^3 + y^3 = 189 \cdot z^3$$
$$= 148^3 + 185^3 = 189 \cdot 37^3 = 9573417$$

Solution 1:

$$x = 148, y = 185, z = 37$$

The second approach to

$$\zeta(s)_2 = 6^3 + (-3)^3 = 189$$

$$x = 6 \cdot z$$
$$y = -3 \cdot z$$

The values of x, y

$$z = 37$$
$$x = 6 \cdot z = 6 \cdot 37 = 222$$
$$y = -3 \cdot z = -3 \cdot 37 = -111$$

Replace these values into $F_2(s)$

Try again

$$F_2(s) = x^3 + y^3 = 189 \cdot z^3$$
$$= 222^3 + (-111)^3 = 189 \cdot 37^3 = 9573417$$

Solution 2:

$$x = 222, y = -111, z = 37$$

From $F_1(s)$ and $F_2(s)$ we have

$$148^3 + 185^3 = 222^3 + (-111)^3 = 91 \cdot 17^3$$
$$= 447083$$

Or $148^3 + 185^3 = 222^3 + (-111)^3$

Then

$$111^3 + 148^3 + 185^3 = 222^3$$

Back to the Fermat-Wiles Equation below

$$x^3 + y^3 = 217 \cdot z^3$$
$$\zeta(s) = c \text{ and } \zeta(c) = 0$$

Find the values of r, s

$$r^3 + s^3 = 217$$
$$c = 217$$
$$\zeta(s) = r^3 + s^3 = 217$$
$$\zeta(s)_1 = 6^3 + 1^3 = 217$$
$$\zeta(s)_2 = 9^3 + (-8)^3 = 217$$

The first approach to

$$\zeta(s) = 6^3 + 1^3 = 217$$

$$x = 6 \cdot z$$
$$y = 1 \cdot z$$

The values of x, y

Choose any value of z (z = 73)

$$x = 6 \cdot z = 6 \cdot 73 = 438$$
$$y = 1 \cdot z = 1 \cdot 73 = 73$$

Replace these values into $F_1(s)$

Try again

$$F_1(s) = x^3 + y^3 = 217 \cdot z^3$$
$$= 438^3 + 73^3 = 217 \cdot 73^3 = 84416689$$

Solution 1:

$$x = 438, \ y = 73, \ z = 73$$

The second approach to

$$\zeta(s)_2 = 9^3 + (-8)^3 = 217$$

$$x = 9 \cdot z$$
$$y = -8 \cdot z$$

The values of x, y

$$z = 73$$
$$x = 9 \cdot z = 9 \cdot 73 = 657$$
$$y = -8 \cdot z = -8 \cdot 73 = -584$$

Replace these values into $F_2(s)$

Try again

$$F_2(s) = x^3 + y^3 = 217 \cdot z^3$$
$$= 657^3 + (-584)^3 = 217 \cdot 73^3 = 84416689$$

Solution 2:

$$x = 657, y = -584, z = 73$$

From $F_1(s)$ and $F_2(s)$ we have

$$438^3 + 73^3 = 657^3 + (-584)^3 = 217 \cdot 73^3$$
$$= 84416689$$
$$\text{Or } 438^3 + 73^3 = 657^3 + (-584)^3$$

Then

$$584^3 + 438^3 + 73^3 = 657^3$$

Solution:

The values of a, b, c, d

$$51^3 + 68^3 + 85^3 = 102^3$$
$$111^3 + 148^3 + 185^3 = 222^3$$
$$584^3 + 438^3 + 73^3 = 657^3$$

...

_____

*) Find the values of a, b, c, d of the Diophantine equation below

$$a^3 + b^3 + c^3 = d^3$$

Unknowns take the whole numbers

Given: the smallest value has 3 digits

Solve

Used the popular methods to find values a, b, c, d as follows

$$\zeta(s) = r^n + s^n = c$$

$$s = \sqrt[n]{c - r^n}$$
$$r = \sqrt[n]{c - s^n}$$
$$\zeta(s) = c \ \& \ \zeta(c) = 0$$
$$x = r \cdot z = \sqrt[n]{c - s^n \cdot z}$$
$$y = s \cdot z = \sqrt[n]{c - r^n \cdot z}$$

$$n \to \infty$$

There are many values of r and s as following

$$\zeta_1(s) = r^n + s^n = c$$

$$\zeta_1(s) = r^3 + s^3 = 721$$
$$16^3 + (-15)^3 = 721$$

And

$$\zeta_2(s) = r^n + s^n = c$$

$$\zeta_2(s) = r^3 + s^3 = 721$$
$$9^3 + (-2)^3 = 721$$

Or

$$\zeta_1(s) = r^n + s^n = c$$

$$\zeta_1(s) = r^3 + s^3 = 1729$$
$$9^3 + 10^3 = 1729$$

And

$$\zeta_2(s) = r^n + s^n = c$$

$$\zeta_2(s) = r^3 + s^3 = 721$$
$$12^3 + 1^3 = 1729$$

Or

$$\zeta_1(s) = r^n + s^n = c$$

$$\zeta_1(s) = r^3 + s^3 = 152$$
$$3^3 + 5^3 = 152$$

And

$$\zeta_2(s) = r^n + s^n = c$$

$$\zeta_2(s) = r^3 + s^3 = 152$$
$$6^3 + (-4)^3 = 152$$

The second we use the popular method for to find the values of a, b, c, and d

$$\zeta(s) = r^n + s^n = c$$

$$s = \sqrt[n]{c - r^n}$$
$$r = \sqrt[n]{c - s^n}$$
$$\zeta(s) = c \ \& \ \zeta(c) = 0$$
$$x = r \cdot z = \sqrt[n]{c - s^n} \cdot z$$
$$y = s \cdot z = \sqrt[n]{c - r^n} \cdot z$$

$$n \to \infty$$

Back to the Fermat-Wiles Equation below

$$x^3 + y^3 = 721 \cdot z^3$$

157

The values of x, y, z

$$\zeta(s) = c \text{ and } \zeta(c) = 0$$

Find the values of r, s

$$r^3 + s^3 = c$$

$$c = 721$$

$$\zeta(s) = r^3 + s^3 = 721$$

$$\zeta(s)_1 = 16^3 + (-15)^3 = 721$$

$$\zeta(s)_2 = 9^3 + (-2)^3 = 721$$

The first approach to

$$\zeta(s) = 16^3 + (-15)^3 = 721$$

$$x = 16 \cdot z$$

$$y = -15 \cdot z$$

The values of x, y

Choose any value of z (z = 337)

$$x = 16 \cdot z = 16 \cdot 337 = 5392$$

$$y = -15 \cdot z = -15 \cdot 337 = -5055$$

Replace these values into $F_1(s)$

Try again

$$F_1(s) = x^3 + y^3 = 721 \cdot z^3$$

$$= 5392^3 + (-5055)^3 = 721 \cdot 337^3$$

$$= 27594654913$$

Solution 1:

$$x = 5392, y = -5055, z = 337$$

The second approach to

$$\zeta(s)_2 = 9^3 + (-2)^3 = 721$$

$$x = 9 \cdot z$$
$$y = -2 \cdot z$$

The values of x, y

$$z = 337$$
$$x = 9 \cdot z = 9 \cdot 337 = 3033$$
$$y = -2 \cdot z = -2 \cdot 337 = -674$$

Replace these values into $F_2(s)$

Try again

$$F_2(s) = x^3 + y^3 = 721 \cdot z^3$$
$$= 3033^3 + (-674)^3 = 721 \cdot 337^3 = 27594654913$$

Solution 2:

$$x = 3033, y = -674, z = 337$$

From $F_1(s)$ and $F_2(s)$ we have

$$5392^3 + (-5055)^3 = 3033^3 + (-674)^3 = 721 \cdot 337^3$$
$$= 27594654913$$

Or $5392^3 + (-5055)^3 = 3033^3 + (-674)^3$

Then

$$3033^3 + 5055^3 + (-674)^3 = 5392^3$$

Back to the Fermat-Wiles Equation below

$$x^3 + y^3 = 1729 \cdot z^3$$
$$\zeta(s) = c \text{ and } \zeta(c) = 0$$

Find the values of r, s

$$r^3 + s^3 = c$$
$$c = 1729$$
$$\zeta(s) = r^3 + s^3 = 1729$$
$$\zeta(s)_1 = 9^3 + 10^3 = 1729$$
$$\zeta(s)_2 = 12^3 + 1^3 = 1729$$

The first approach to

$$\zeta(s) = 9^3 + 10^3 = 1729$$

$$x = 9 \cdot z$$
$$y = 10 \cdot z$$

The values of x, y

Choose any value of z (z = 199)

$$x = 9 \cdot z = 9 \cdot 199 = 1791$$
$$y = 10 \cdot z = 10 \cdot 199 = 1990$$

Replace these values into $F_1(s)$

Try again

$$F_1(s) = x^3 + y^3 = 1729 \cdot z^3$$
$$= 1791^3 + 1990^3 = 1729 \cdot 199^3 = 13625555671$$

Solution 1:

$$x = 1791, y = 1990, z = 199$$

The second approach to

$$\zeta(s)_2 = 12^3 + 1^3 = 1729$$

$$x = 12 \cdot z$$
$$y = 1 \cdot z$$

The values of x, y

$$z = 199$$
$$x = 12 \cdot z = 12 \cdot 199 = 2388$$
$$y = 1 \cdot z = 1 \cdot 199 = 199$$

Replace these values into $F_2(s)$

Try again

$$F_2(s) = x^3 + y^3 = 1729 \cdot z^3$$
$$= 2388^3 + 199^3 = 1729 \cdot 199^3 = 13625555671$$

Solution 2:

$$x = 2388, y = 199, z = 199$$

From $F_1(s)$ and $F_2(s)$ we have

$$1791^3 + 1990^3 = 2388^3 + 199^3 = 1729 \cdot 199^3$$
$$= 13625555671$$

Or

$$1791^3 + 1990^3 = 2388^3 + 199^3$$

Then

$$1791^3 + 1990^3 - 199^3 = 2388^3$$

Back to the Fermat-Wiles Equation below

$$x^3 + y^3 = 152 \cdot z^3$$
$$\zeta(s) = c \text{ and } \zeta(c) = 0$$

Find the values of r, s

$$r^3 + s^3 = c$$
$$c = 152$$
$$\zeta(s) = r^3 + s^3 = 152$$
$$\zeta(s)_1 = 3^3 + 5^3 = 152$$
$$\zeta(s)_2 = 6^3 + (-4)^3 = 152$$

The first approach to

$$\zeta(s) = 3^3 + 5^3 = 152$$

$$x = 3 \cdot z$$
$$y = 5 \cdot z$$

The values of x, y

Choose any value of z (z = 367)

$$x = 3 \cdot z = 3 \cdot 367 = 1101$$
$$y = 5 \cdot z = 5 \cdot 367 = 1835$$

Replace these values into $F_1(s)$

Try again

$$F_1(s) = x^3 + y^3 = 152 \cdot z^3$$
$$= 1101^3 + 1835^3 = 152 \cdot 367^3 = 7513491176$$

Solution 1:

$$x = 1101, y = 1835, z = 367$$

The second approach to

$$\zeta(s)_2 = 6^3 + (-4)^3 = 152$$

$$x = 6 \cdot z$$
$$y = -4 \cdot z$$

The values of x, y

$$z = 367$$
$$x = 6 \cdot z = 6 \cdot 367 = 2202$$
$$y = -4 \cdot z = -4 \cdot 367 = -1468$$

Replace these values into $F_2(s)$

Try again

$$F_2(s) = x^3 + y^3 = 152 \cdot z^3$$
$$= 2202^3 + (-1468)^3 = 152 \cdot 367^3$$
$$= 7513491176$$

Solution 2:

$$x = 2202, \ y = -1468, \ z = 367$$

From $F_1(s)$ and $F_2(s)$ we have

$$1101^3 + 1835^3 = 2202^3 + (-1468)^3 = 152 \cdot 367^3$$
$$= 7513491176$$

Or

$$1101^3 + 1835^3 = 2202^3 + (-1468)^3$$

Then

$$1101^3 + 1468^3 + 1835^3 = 2202^3$$

Solution: The values of a, b, c, d

$$3033^3 + 5055^3 - 674^3 = 5392^3$$
$$1791^3 + 1990^3 - 199^3 = 2388^3$$
$$1101^3 + 1468^3 + 1835^3 = 2202^3$$

...

_____

EXERCISES

*) Find the values of a, b, c, d of the Diophantine equation below

$$a^3 + b^3 + c^3 = d^3$$

Unknowns take the whole numbers

The smallest value has 2 digits

*) Find the values of a, b, c, d of the Diophantine equation below

$$a^3 + b^3 + c^3 = d^3$$

Unknowns take the whole numbers

The smallest value has 3 digits

*) Find the values of a, b, c, d of the Diophantine equation below

$$a^3 + b^3 + c^3 = d^3$$

Unknowns take the whole numbers
The smallest value has 3 digits

*) Find the values of a, b, c, d of the Diophantine equation below

$$a^3 + b^3 + c^3 = d^3$$

Unknowns take the whole numbers

The smallest value has 3 digits

*) Find the values of a, b, c, d of the Diophantine equation below

$$a^3 + b^3 + c^3 = d^3$$

Unknowns take the whole numbers

The smallest value has 4 digits

*) Find the values of a, b, c, d of the Diophantine equation below

$$a^3 + b^3 + c^3 = d^3$$

Unknowns take the whole numbers

The smallest value has 4 digits

*) Find the values of a, b, c, d of the Diophantine equation below

$$a^3 + b^3 + c^3 = d^3$$

Unknowns take the whole numbers

The smallest value has 5 digits

*) Find the values of a, b, c, d of the Diophantine equation below

$$a^3 + b^3 + c^3 = d^3$$

Unknowns take the whole numbers

The smallest value has 5 digits and

*) Find the values of a, b, c, d of the Diophantine equation below

$$a^3 + b^3 + c^3 = d^3$$

Unknowns take the whole numbers

The smallest value has 6 digits

*) Find the values of a, b, c, d of the Diophantine equation below

$$a^3 + b^3 + c^3 = d^3$$

Unknowns take the whole numbers

The smallest value has 6 digits

*) Find the values of a, b, c, d of the Diophantine equation below

$$a^3 + b^3 + c^3 = d^3$$

Unknowns take the whole numbers

The smallest value has 7 digits

*) Find the values of a, b, c, d of the Diophantine equation below

$$a^3 + b^3 + c^3 = d^3$$

Unknowns take the whole numbers

The smallest value has 7 digits

*) Find the values of a, b, c, d of the Diophantine equation below

$$a^3 + b^3 + c^3 = d^3$$

Unknowns take the whole numbers

The smallest value has 8 digits

*) Find the values of a, b, c, d of the Diophantine equation below

$$a^3 + b^3 + c^3 = d^3$$

Unknowns take the whole numbers

The smallest value has 8 digits

*) Find the values of a, b, c, d of the Diophantine equation below

$$a^3 + b^3 + c^3 = d^3$$

Unknowns take the whole numbers

The smallest value has 9 digits

*) Find the values of a, b, c, d of the Diophantine equation below

$$a^3 + b^3 + c^3 = d^3$$

Unknowns take the whole numbers

The smallest value has 9 digits

*) Find the values of a, b, c, d of the Diophantine equation below

$$a^3 + b^3 + c^3 = d^3$$

Unknowns take the whole numbers

The smallest value has 10 digits

EXPAND DIOPHANTINE EQUATIONS
$$a^3 + b^3 + c^3 + d^3 = e^3$$

Expanded from 3 unknowns of the Fermat-Wiles equation to Diophantine equation gets 5 unknowns

Example:

*) Find the values of a, b, c, d, e of the Diophantine equation below

$$a^3 + b^3 + c^3 + d^3 = e^3$$

Unknowns take the whole numbers place

Given Info: the smallest value has 3 digits

Solve

Similarly, we use the popular method to find the values of a, b, c, d, and e as following:

$$\zeta(s) = r^n + s^n = c$$

$$s = \sqrt[n]{c - r^n}$$
$$r = \sqrt[n]{c - s^n}$$
$$\zeta(s) = c \; \& \; \zeta(c) = 0$$
$$x = r \cdot z = \sqrt[n]{c - s^n} \cdot z$$
$$y = s \cdot z = \sqrt[n]{c - r^n} \cdot z$$
$$n \rightarrow \infty$$

There are many values of r, s, and more as following

$$\zeta_1(s) = r^n + s^n = c$$

$$\zeta_1(s) = r^3 + s^3 = 397$$
$$12^3 + (-11)^3 = 397$$

And

$$\zeta_2(s) = r^n + s^n + t^n = c$$

$$\zeta_2(s) = r^3 + s^3 + t^3 = c$$
$$7^3 + 3^3 + 3^3 = 397$$

Second we use the popular method for to find the values of a, b, c, d and e:

$$\zeta(s) = r^n + s^n = c$$

$$s = \sqrt[n]{c - r^n}$$

$$r=\sqrt[n]{c-s^n}$$
$$\zeta(s)=c \ \& \ \zeta(c)=0$$
$$x=r\cdot z=\sqrt[n]{c-s^n\cdot z}$$
$$y=s\cdot z=\sqrt[n]{c-r^n\cdot z}$$
$$n\to\infty$$

Back to the Fermat-Wiles Equation

We get 2 equations
$$F_1(s) = x^3 + y^3 = 397\cdot z^3$$
$$F_2(s) = v^3 + x^3 + y^3 = \cdot z^3$$

The values of v, x, y, z

The first step

Find the values x, y of $F_1(s)$

Similarly $\zeta(s) = c$ and $\zeta(c) = 0$
The values of r, s of $F_1(s)$
$$c = 397$$
$$\zeta(s)_1 = r^3 + s^3 = 397$$
$$\zeta(s)_1 = 12^3 + (-11)^3 = 397$$

Then
$$x = r\cdot z$$
$$y = s\cdot z$$

The values of x, y

Choose any value of z (z = 193)

$$x = r \cdot z = 12 \cdot 193 = 2316$$
$$y = s \cdot z = -11 \cdot 193 = -2123$$

Replace these values into $F_1(s)$

Try again

$$F_1(s) = x^3 + y^3 = 397 \cdot z^3$$
$$F_1(s) = 2316^3 + (-2123)^3 = 397 \cdot 193^3$$
$$= 2854055629$$

Solution 1:

$$x = 2316, \ y = -2123, \ z = 193$$

Next step

Find the values v, x, y of $F_2(s)$

Similarly $\zeta(s) = c$ and $\zeta(c) = 0$

Find the values of r, s, t of $F_2(s)$

$$\zeta(s)_2 = r^3 + s^3 + t^3 = 397$$
$$\zeta(s)_2 = 7^3 + 3^3 + 3^3 = 397$$

Then

$$v = r \cdot z$$
$$x = s \cdot z$$
$$y = t \cdot z$$

The values of v, x, y

$$z = 193$$
$$v = r \cdot z = 7 \cdot 193 = 1351$$
$$x = s \cdot z = 3 \cdot 193 = 579$$
$$y = t \cdot z = 3 \cdot 193 = 579$$

Replace these values into $F_2(s)$

Try again

$$F_2(s) = v^3 + x^3 + y^3 = 397 \cdot z^3$$
$$F_2(s) = 1351^3 + 579^3 + 579^3 = 397 \cdot 193^3$$
$$= 2854055629$$

Solution 2:

$$v = 1351, x = 579, y = 579, z = 193$$

From $F_1(s)$ and $F_2(s)$ we have

$$2316^3 + (-2123)^3 = 1351^3 + 579^3 + 579^3 = 397 \cdot 193^3$$

Or $2316^3 + (-2123)^3 = 1351^3 + 579^3 + 579^3$

Then

$$2123^3 + 1351^3 + 579^3 + 579^3 = 2316^3$$

Soluion:

$$2123^3 + 1351^3 + 579^3 + 579^3 = 2316^3$$

*) Find the values of a, b, c, d, e of the Diophantine equation below

$$a^3 + b^3 + c^3 + d^3 = e^3$$

Unknowns take the whole numbers

Given: the smallest value has 3 digits

Solve

Similarly we use the popular method to find the values a, b, c, d, e as following

$$\zeta(s) = r^n + s^n = c$$

$$s = \sqrt[n]{c - r^n}$$
$$r = \sqrt[n]{c - s^n}$$
$$\zeta(s) = c \ \& \ \zeta(c) = 0$$
$$x = r \cdot z = \sqrt[n]{c - s^n} \cdot z$$
$$y = s \cdot z = \sqrt[n]{c - r^n} \cdot z$$

$$n \to \infty$$

The values of r, s, t as following

$$\zeta_1(s) = r^n + s^n = c$$

$$\zeta_1(s) = r^3 + s^3 = 547$$
$$14^3 + (-13)^3 = 547$$

And

$$\zeta_2(s) = r^n + s^n + t^n = c$$
$$\zeta_2(s) = r^3 + s^3 + t^3 = c$$
$$8^3 + 3^3 + 2^3 = 547$$

The second we use the popular method for to find the values of a, b, c, d and e

$$\zeta(s) = r^n + s^n = c$$

$$s = \sqrt[n]{c - r^n}$$
$$r = \sqrt[n]{c - s^n}$$
$$\zeta(s) = c \ \& \ \zeta(c) = 0$$
$$x = r \cdot z = \sqrt[n]{c - s^n \cdot z}$$
$$y = s \cdot z = \sqrt[n]{c - r^n \cdot z}$$

$$n \to \infty$$

Back to the Fermat-Wiles Equation below

$$F_1(s) = x^3 + y^3 = 547 \cdot z^3$$
$$F_2(s) = v^3 + x^3 + y^3 = 547 \cdot z^3$$

The first step

Find the values x, y of $F_1(s)$

Similarly $\zeta(s) = c$ and $\zeta(c) = 0$

The values of r, s of $F_1(s)$

$$c = 547$$
$$\zeta(s)_1 = r^3 + s^3 = 547$$
$$\zeta(s)_1 = 14^3 + (-13)^3 = 547$$

Then

$$x = r \cdot z$$
$$y = s \cdot z$$

The values of x, y

Choose any value of z (z = 167)

$$x = r \cdot z = 14 \cdot 167 = 2338$$
$$y = s \cdot z = -13 \cdot 167 = -2171$$

Replace these values into $F_1(s)$

Try again

$$F_1(s) = x^3 + y^3 = 547 \cdot z^3$$
$$F_1(s) = 2338^3 + (-2171)^3 = 547 \cdot 167^3$$
$$= 2547632261$$

Solution 1:

$$x = 2338, \; y = -2171, \; z = 167$$

Next step

Find the values v, x, y of $F_2(s)$

Similarly $\zeta(s) = c$ and $\zeta(c) = 0$

Find the values of r, s, t of $F_2(s)$

$$\zeta(s)_2 = r^3 + s^3 + t^3 = 547$$
$$\zeta(s)_2 = 8^3 + 3^3 + 2^3 = 547$$

Then

$$v = r \cdot z$$
$$x = s \cdot z$$
$$y = t \cdot z$$

The values of v, x, y

$$z = 167$$
$$v = r \cdot z = 8 \cdot 167 = 1336$$
$$x = s \cdot z = 3 \cdot 167 = 501$$
$$y = t \cdot z = 2 \cdot 167 = 334$$

Replace these values into $F_2(s)$

Try again

$$F_2(s) = v^3 + x^3 + y^3 = 547 \cdot z^3$$
$$F_2(s) = 1336^3 + 501^3 + 334^3 = 547 \cdot 167^3$$
$$= 2547632261$$

Solution 2:

$$v = 1336, x = 501, y = 334, z = 167$$

From $F_1(s)$ and $F_2(s)$ we have

$$2338^3 + (-2171)^3 = 1336^3 + 501^3 + 334^3 = 547 \cdot 167^3$$

Or

$$2338^3 + (-2171)^3 = 1336^3 + 501^3 + 334^3$$

Then

$$2171^3 + 1336^3 + 501^3 + 334^3 = 2338^3$$

Solution:

$$2171^3 + 1336^3 + 501^3 + 334^3 = 2338^3$$

---

*) Find the values of a, b, c, d, e of the Diophantine equation below

$$a^3 + b^3 + c^3 + d^3 = e^3$$

Unknowns take the whole numbers

Given: the smallest value has 3 digits

Solve

Similarly we use the popular method to find the values a, b, c, d, e as following

$$\zeta(s) = r^n + s^n = c$$

$$s = \sqrt{c - r}$$

$$r = \sqrt[n]{c - s^n}$$

$$\zeta(s) = c \ \& \ \zeta(c) = 0$$

$$x = r \cdot z = \sqrt[n]{c - s^n \cdot z}$$

$$y = s \cdot z = \sqrt[n]{c - r^n \cdot z}$$

$$n \to \infty$$

The values of r, s, t as following

$$\zeta_1(s) = r^n + s^n = c$$

$$\zeta_1(s) = r^3 + s^3 = 1197$$
$$13^3 + (-10)^3 = 1197$$

And

$$\zeta_2(s) = r^n + s^n + t^n = c$$

$$\zeta_2(s) = r^3 + s^3 + t^3 = c$$
$$9^3 + 7^3 + 5^3 = 1197$$

The second we use the popular method for to find the values of a, b, c, d and e

$$\zeta(s) = r^n + s^n = c$$

$$s = \sqrt[n]{c - r^n}$$
$$r = \sqrt[n]{c - s^n}$$
$$\zeta(s) = c \ \& \ \zeta(c) = 0$$
$$x = r \cdot z = \sqrt[n]{c - s^n \cdot z}$$
$$y = s \cdot z = \sqrt[n]{c - r^n \cdot z}$$
$$n \to \infty$$

Back to the Fermat-Wiles Equation below

$$F_1(s) = x^3 + y^3 = 1197 \cdot z^3$$
$$F_2(s) = v^3 + x^3 + y^3 = 1197 \cdot z^3$$

The first step

Find the values x, y of $F_1(s)$

Similarly $\zeta(s) = c$ and $\zeta(c) = 0$

The values of r, s of $F_1(s)$

$$c = 1197$$

$$\zeta(s)_1 = r^3 + s^3 = 1197$$
$$\zeta(s)_1 = 13^3 + (-10)^3 = 1197$$

Then

$$x = r \cdot z$$
$$y = s \cdot z$$

The values of x, y

Choose any value of z (z = 311)

$$x = r \cdot z = 13 \cdot 311 = 4043$$
$$y = s \cdot z = -10 \cdot 311 = -3110$$

Replace these values into $F_1(s)$

Try again

$$F_1(s) = x^3 + y^3 = 1197 \cdot z^3$$
$$F_1(s) = 4043^3 + (-3110)^3 = 1197 \cdot 311^3$$
$$= 36006036507$$

Solution 1:

$$x = 4043, y = -3110, z = 311$$

The next step

Finding the values v, x, y of $F_2(s)$
Similarly $\zeta(s) = c$ and $\zeta(c) = 0$
Find the values of r, s, t of $F_2(s)$

$$\zeta(s)_2 = r^3 + s^3 + t^3 = 1197$$
$$\zeta(s)_2 = 9^3 + 7^3 + 5^3 = 1197$$

Then

$$v = r \cdot z$$
$$x = s \cdot z$$
$$y = t \cdot z$$

The values of v, x, y

$$z = 311$$
$$v = r \cdot z = 9 \cdot 311 = 2799$$
$$x = s \cdot z = 7 \cdot 311 = 2177$$
$$y = t \cdot z = 5 \cdot 311 = 1555$$

Replace these values into $F_2(s)$
Try again

$$F_2(s) = v^3 + x^3 + y^3 = 1197 \cdot z^3$$
$$F_2(s) = 2799^3 + 2177^3 + 1555^3 = 1197 \cdot 311^3$$
$$= 36006036507$$

Solution 2:

$$v = 2799, x = 2177, y = 1555, z = 311$$

From $F_1(s)$ and $F_2(s)$ we have

$$4043^3 + (-3110)^3 = 2799^3 + 2177^3 + 1555^3 = 1197 \cdot 311^3$$

Or

$$4043^3 + (-3110)^3 = 2799^3 + 2177^3 + 1555^3$$

Then

$$3110^3 + 2799^3 + 2177^3 + 1555^3 = 4043^3$$

Solution:

$$3110^3 + 2799^3 + 2177^3 + 1555^3 = 4043^3$$

EXERCISES

*) Find the values of a, b, c, d, e of the Diophantine equation below

$$a^3 + b^3 + c^3 + d^3 = e^3$$

Unknowns take the whole numbers

Given: the smallest value has 2 digits

*) Find the values of a, b, c, d, e of the Diophantine equation below

$$a^3 + b^3 + c^3 + d^3 = e^3$$

Unknowns take the whole numbers

Given: the smallest value has 2 digits

*) Find the values of a, b, c, d, e of the Diophantine equation below

$$a^3 + b^3 + c^3 + d^3 = e^3$$

Unknowns take the whole numbers

Given: the smallest value has 3 digits

*) Find the values of a, b, c, d, e of the Diophantine equation below

$$a^3 + b^3 + c^3 + d^3 = e^3$$

Unknowns take the whole numbers

Given: the smallest value has 3 digits

*) Find the values of a, b, c, d, e of the Diophantine equation below

$$a^3 + b^3 + c^3 + d^3 = e^3$$

Unknowns take the whole numbers

Given: the smallest value has 3 digits

*) Find the values of a, b, c, d, e of the Diophantine equation below

$$a^3 + b^3 + c^3 + d^3 = e^3$$

Unknowns take the whole numbers

Given: the smallest value has 4 digits

*) Find the values of a, b, c, d, e of the Diophantine equation below

$$a^3 + b^3 + c^3 + d^3 = e^3$$

Unknowns take the whole numbers

Given: the smallest value has 4 digits

*) Find the values of a, b, c, d, e of the Diophantine equation below

$$a^3 + b^3 + c^3 + d^3 = e^3$$

Unknowns take the whole numbers

Given: the smallest value has 4 digits

*) Find the values of a, b, c, d of the Diophantine equation below

$$a^3 + b^3 + c^3 + d^3 = e^3$$

Unknowns take the whole numbers

Given: the smallest value has 5 digits

*) Find the values of a, b, c, d, e of the Diophantine equation below

$$a^3 + b^3 + c^3 + d^3 = e^3$$

Unknowns take the whole numbers

Given: the smallest value has 5 digits

*) Find the values of a, b, c, d, e of the Diophantine equation below

$$a^3 + b^3 + c^3 + d^3 = e^3$$

Unknowns take the whole numbers

Given: the smallest value has 6 digits

*) Find the values of a, b, c, d, e of the Diophantine equation below

$$a^3 + b^3 + c^3 + d^3 = e^3$$

Unknowns take the whole numbers

Given: the smallest value has 6 digits

*) Find the values of a, b, c, d, e of the Diophantine equation below

$$a^3 + b^3 + c^3 + d^3 = e^3$$

Unknowns take the whole numbers

Given: the smallest value has 6 digits

*) Find the values of a, b, c, d, e of the Diophantine equation below

$$a^3 + b^3 + c^3 + d^3 = e^3$$

Unknowns take the whole numbers

Given: the smallest value has 7 digits

*) Find the values of a, b, c, d, e of the Diophantine equation below

$$a^3 + b^3 + c^3 + d^3 = e^3$$

Unknowns take the whole numbers

Given: the smallest value has 7 digits

*) Find the values of a, b, c, d, e of the Diophantine equation below

$$a^3 + b^3 + c^3 + d^3 = e^3$$

Unknowns take the whole numbers

Given: the smallest value has 8 digits

*) Find the values of a, b, c, d, e of the Diophantine equation below

$$a^3 + b^3 + c^3 + d^3 = e^3$$

Unknowns take the whole numbers

Given: the smallest value has 8 digits

EXPANSION FERMAT-WILES EQUATION
$$v^3 + x^3 + y^3 = d \cdot z^3$$

I am applying my popular method for the Diophantine equation, which takes the form
$$v^3 + x^3 + y^3 = d \cdot z^3$$

Unknowns take the whole numbers

Solve

Applying the popular method:
$$\zeta(s) = r^3 + s^3 + t^3 = d$$

And
$$\zeta(s) = d \text{ and } \zeta(d) = 0,$$

The values of r, s and t, as the table below:

3, 10, 17, 24, 43, 62, 66, 73, 80, 81, 92, 99, 118, 127, 129, 134, 136, …

Next step

Applying the popular method below

$$\zeta(s) = r^n + s^n = c$$

$$s = \sqrt[n]{c - r^n}$$
$$r = \sqrt[n]{c - s^n}$$
$$\zeta(s) = c \ \& \ \zeta(c) = 0$$
$$x = r \cdot z = \sqrt[n]{c - s^n \cdot z}$$
$$y = s \cdot z = \sqrt[n]{c - r^n \cdot z}$$

$$n \to \infty$$

We get:

$$\zeta(s) = r^3 + s^3 + t^3 = d$$
$$\zeta(s) = d \text{ and } \zeta(d) = 0$$

$$A = r \cdot D$$
$$B = s \cdot D$$
$$C = t \cdot D$$

~~~~~~~~/////~~~~~~~

*) There are 204 candies in candy box, which get four different colors: red, blue, yellow and purple

If cubes of the red, blue, and yellow candies, then sum all of three, it's equal to multiple 251 by the cubes purple candies

How many candies of each color?

Solve

We put

A= red candy

B = green candy,

C = yellow candy

D = purple candy

We have

$$F_1(s) = A + B + C + D = 204$$
$$F_2(s) = A^3 + B^3 + C^3 = 251 \cdot D^3$$

Back to Fermat Wiles equaion

$$x^n + y^n = c \cdot z^n$$

Applying the popular method, n = 3

$$\zeta(s) = r^n + s^n = c$$

$$s = \sqrt[n]{c - r^n}$$
$$r = \sqrt[n]{c - s^n}$$
$$\zeta(s) = c \ \& \ \zeta(c) = 0$$
$$x = r \cdot z = \sqrt[n]{c - s^n} \cdot z$$
$$y = s \cdot z = \sqrt[n]{c - r^n} \cdot z$$

$$n \to \infty$$

The values of A, B, C, d

$$\zeta(s) = d \text{ and } \zeta(d) = 0$$
$$F_2(s) = A^3 + B^3 + C^3 = d \cdot D^3$$

Find the values of r, s, t

$$d = 251$$

$$\zeta(s) = r^3 + s^3 + t^3 = d = 251$$

$$\zeta(s)_1 = 2^3 + 3^3 + 6^3 = 251$$

$$\zeta(s)_2 = 1^3 + 5^3 + 5^3 = 251$$

The first approach to

$$\zeta(s)_1 = 2^3 + 3^3 + 6^3 = 251$$

$$A = r \cdot D$$

$$B = s \cdot D$$

$$C = t \cdot D$$

The value of D

We have

$$F_1(s) = A + B + C + D = 204$$

And

$$r + s + t = 2 + 3 + 6 = 11$$

Then

$$D = \frac{204}{r+s+t+1} = \frac{204}{12} = 17$$

The values of A, B, C

D = 17 candies

$$A = r \cdot D = 2 \cdot 17 = 34 \text{ candies}$$

$$B = s \cdot D = 3 \cdot 17 = 51 \text{ candies}$$

$$C = t \cdot D = 6 \cdot 17 = 102 \text{ candies}$$

192

Replace these values into F(s)

Try again

$$F_1(s) = A + B + C + D = 204$$
$$F_1(s) = 34 + 51 + 102 + 17 = 204$$

And

$$F_2(s) = A^3 + B^3 + C^3 = 251 \cdot D^3$$
$$F_2(s) = 34^3 + 51^3 + 102^3 = 251 \cdot 17^3 = 1233163$$

Solution 1:

$$D = 17 \text{ candies}$$
$$A = 34 \text{ candies}$$
$$B = 51 \text{ candies}$$
$$C = 102 \text{ candies}$$

The second approach to

$$\zeta(s)_2 = 1^3 + 5^3 + 5^3 = 251$$
$$A = r \cdot D$$
$$B = s \cdot D$$
$$C = t \cdot D$$

The values of A, B, C

$$D = 17 \text{ candies}$$
$$A = r \cdot D = 1 \cdot 17 = 17 \text{ candies}$$
$$B = s \cdot D = 5 \cdot 17 = 85 \text{ candies}$$
$$C = t \cdot D = 5 \cdot 17 = 85 \text{ candies}$$

Replace these values into F(s)

Try again

$$F_1(s) = A + B + C + D = 204$$
$$F_1(s) = 17 + 85 + 85 + 17 = 204$$

And

$$F_2(s) = A^3 + B^3 + C^3 = 251 \cdot D^3$$
$$F_2(s) = 17^3 + 85^3 + 85^3 = 251 \cdot 17^3 = 1233163$$

Solution 2:

D = 17 candies
A = 17 candies
B = 85 candies
C = 85 candies

─────────────────────

*) There are 1680 candies in candy box, which get four different colors: red, blue, yellow and purple

If cubes of the red, blue, and yellow candies, then sum all of three, it's equal to multiple 853 by the cubes purple candies

How many candies of each color?

Solve

We put

A= red candy

B = green candy

C = yellow candy

D = purple candy

According to the problem

$$F_1(s) = A + B + C + D = 1680$$

$$F_2(s) = A^3 + B^3 + C^3 = 853 \cdot D^3$$

Back to Fermat Wiles equaion

$$x^n + y^n = c \cdot z^n$$

Applying the popular method, n = 3

$$\zeta(s) = r^n + s^n = c$$

$$s = \sqrt[n]{c - r^n}$$

$$r = \sqrt[n]{c - s^n}$$

$$\zeta(s) = c \ \& \ \zeta(c) = 0$$

$$x = r \cdot z = \sqrt[n]{c - s^n} \cdot z$$

$$y = s \cdot z = \sqrt[n]{c - r^n} \cdot z$$

$$n \to \infty$$

The values of A, B, C, D, d

$$\zeta(s) = d \text{ and } \zeta(d) = 0$$

$$F_2(s) = A^3 + B^3 + C^3 = d \cdot D^3$$

Find the values of r, s, t

$$d = 853$$

$$\zeta(s) = r^3 + s^3 + t^3 = d = 853$$

$$\zeta(s)_1 = 5^3 + 6^3 + 8^3 = 853$$

$$\zeta(s)_2 = 9^3 + 5^3 + (-1)^3 = 853$$

The first approach to

$$\zeta(s)_1 = 5^3 + 6^3 + 8^3 = 853$$

$$A = r \cdot D$$

$$B = s \cdot D$$

$$C = t \cdot D$$

The value of D

We have

$$A + B + C + D = 1680$$

And

$$r + s + t = 5 + 6 + 8 = 19$$

Then

$$\frac{1680}{r + s + t +} = \frac{1680}{20} = 84$$

The values of A, B, C

$$D = 84 \text{ candies}$$

$$A = r \cdot D = 5 \cdot 84 = 420 \text{ candies}$$

$$B = s \cdot D = 6 \cdot 84 = 504 \text{ candies}$$

$$C = t \cdot D = 8 \cdot 84 = 672 \text{ candies}$$

Replace these values into F(s)

Try again

$$F_1(s) = A + B + C + D = 1680$$

$$F_1(s) = 420 + 504 + 672 + 84 = 1680$$

And

$$F_2(s) = A^3 + B^3 + C^3 = 853 \cdot D^3$$
$$F_2(s) = 420^3 + 504^3 + 672^3 = 853 \cdot 84^3 = 505576512$$

Solution 1:

$$D = 84 \text{ candies}$$
$$A = 420 \text{ candies}$$
$$B = 504 \text{ candies}$$
$$C = 672 \text{ candies}$$

The second approach to

$$\zeta(s)_2 = 9^3 + 5^3 + (-1)^3 = 853$$
$$A = r \cdot D$$
$$B = s \cdot D$$
$$C = t \cdot D$$

The value of D

We have

$$F_1(s) = A + B + C + D = 1680$$

And

$$r + s + t = 9 + 5 + (-1) = 13$$

Then

$$D = \frac{1680}{r+s+t+1} = \frac{1680}{14} = 120$$

The values of A, B, C

$$D = 120 \text{ candies}$$
$$A = r \cdot D = 9 \cdot 120 = 1080 \text{ candies}$$
$$B = s \cdot D = 5 \cdot 120 = 600 \text{ candies}$$
$$C = t \cdot D = -1 \cdot 120 = -120 \text{ candies (we do not get)}$$

EXERCISES

*) There are 324 candies in candy box, which get four different colors: red, blue, yellow, and purple
If cubes of the red, blue, and yellow candies, then sum all of three, it's equal to multiple 134 by the cubes purple candies

How many candies of each color?

*) There are 286 candies in candy box, which get four different colors: red, blue, yellow, and purple
If cubes of the red, blue, and yellow candies, then sum all of three, it's equal to multiple 244 by the cubes purple candies

How many candies of each color?

*) There are 285 candies in candy box, which get four different colors: red, blue, yellow, and purple
If cubes of the red, blue, and yellow candies, then sum all of three, it's equal to multiple 434 by the cubes purple candies

How many candies of each color?

*) There are 300 candies in candy box, which get four different colors: red, blue, yellow, and purple
If cubes of the red, blue, and yellow candies, then sum all of three, it's equal to multiple 368 by the cubes purple candies

How many candies of each color?

*) There are 450 candies in candy box, which get four different colors: red, blue, yellow, and purple
If cubes of the red, blue, and yellow candies, then sum all of three, it's equal to multiple 476 by the cubes purple candies

How many candies of each color?

*) There are 294 candies in candy box, which get four different colors: red, blue, yellow, and purple
If cubes of the red, blue, and yellow candies, then sum all of three, it's equal to multiple 577 by the cubes purple candies

How many candies of each color?

*) There are 364 candies in candy box, which get four different colors: red, blue, yellow, and purple

If cubes of the red, blue, and yellow candies, then sum all of three, it's equal to multiple 408 by the cubes purple candies

How many candies of each color?

*) There are 570 candies in candy box, which get four different colors: red, blue, yellow, and purple
If cubes of the red, blue, and yellow candies, then sum all of three, it's equal to multiple 638 by the cubes purple candies

How many candies of each color?

*) There are 640 candies in candy box, which get four different colors: red, blue, yellow, and purple
If cubes of the red, blue, and yellow candies, then sum all of three, it's equal to multiple 603 by the cubes purple candies

How many candies of each color?

*) There are 320 candies in candy box, which get four different colors: red, blue, yellow, and purple
If cubes of the red, blue, and yellow candies, then sum all of three, it's equal to multiple 645 by the cubes purple candies

How many candies of each color?

EXPAND DIOPHANTINE EQUATIONS
$$a^3 + b^3 + c^3 + d^3 + e^3 = f^3$$

Expanded from 3 unknowns of the Fermat-Wiles equation to the Diophantine equation get 6 unknowns

Example:

*) Find the values of a, b, c, d, e, and f of the Diophantine equation below
$$a^3 + b^3 + c^3 + d^3 + e^3 = f^3$$
Unknowns take the whole numbers place

Given Info: the smallest value has 3 digits

Solve

Similarly, I am applying my popular method for to find the values a, b, c, d, e, f of the Diophantine equation following:
$$a^3 + b^3 + c^3 + d^3 + e^3 = f^3$$

$$\zeta(s) = r^n + s^n = c$$

$$s=\sqrt[n]{c - r^n}$$
$$r=\sqrt[n]{c - s^n}$$
$$\zeta(s)=c \ \& \ \zeta(c) = 0$$
$$x=r \cdot z=\sqrt[n]{c - s^n \cdot z}$$
$$y=s \cdot z=\sqrt[n]{c - r^n \cdot z}$$

$$n \rightarrow \infty$$

The values of r, s, t, u as following

$$\zeta_1(s) = r^n + s^n = c$$
$$\zeta_1(s) = r^3 + s^3 = 631$$
$$15^3 + (-14)^3 = 631$$

And

$$\zeta_2(s) = r^n + s^n + t^n + u^n = c$$
$$\zeta_2(s) = r^3 + s^3 + t^3 + u^3 = c$$
$$7^3 + 6^3 + 4^3 + 2^3 = 631$$

The next step

Applying the popular method for to find the values of a, b, c, d, e and f

$$\zeta(s) = r^n + s^n = c$$

$$s=\sqrt[n]{c - r^n}$$
$$r=\sqrt[n]{c - s^n}$$
$$\zeta(s)=c \ \& \ \zeta(c) = 0$$
$$x=r \cdot z=\sqrt[n]{c - s^n \cdot z}$$
$$y=s \cdot z=\sqrt[n]{c - r^n \cdot z}$$

$$n \rightarrow \infty$$

Back to the Fermat-Wiles Equation below

$$F_1(s) = x^3 + y^3 = 631 \cdot z^3$$
$$F_2(s) = u^3 + v^3 + x^3 + y^3 = 631 \cdot z^3$$

The values of u, v, x, y, z

The first approach to $F_1(s)$

$$\zeta(s) = c \text{ and } \zeta(c) = 0$$

Find the values of r, s of $F_1(s)$

$$c = 631$$
$$\zeta(s)_1 = r^3 + s^3 = 631$$
$$\zeta(s)_1 = 15^3 + (-14)^3 = 631$$
$$x = r \cdot z$$
$$y = s \cdot z$$

The values of x, y

Choose any value of z (z = 397)

$$x = r \cdot z = 15 \cdot 397 = 5955$$
$$y = s \cdot z = -14 \cdot 397 = -5558$$

Replace these values into $F_1(s)$

Try again

$$F_1(s) = x^3 + y^3 = 631 \cdot z^3$$
$$F_1(s) = 5955^3 + (-5558)^3 = 631 \cdot 397^3$$
$$= 39482157763$$

Solution 1:
$$x = 5955, y = -5558, z = 397$$

The next step to Diophantine equation $F_2(s)$

Find the values of r, s, t, u of $\zeta(s)_2$ of $F_2(s)$

$$\zeta(s)_2 = r^3 + s^3 + t^3 + u^3 = 631$$
$$\zeta(s)_2 = 7^3 + 6^3 + 4^3 + 2^3 = 631$$

Then

$$u = r \cdot z$$
$$v = s \cdot z$$
$$x = t \cdot z$$
$$y = u \cdot z$$

The values of u, v, x, y

$$z = 397$$
$$u = r \cdot z = 7 \cdot 397 = 2779$$
$$v = s \cdot z = 6 \cdot 397 = 2382$$
$$x = t \cdot z = 4 \cdot 397 = 1588$$
$$y = u \cdot z = 2 \cdot 397 = 794$$

Replace these values into $F_2(s)$

Try again

$$F_2(s) = u^3 + v^3 + x^3 + y^3 = 631 \cdot z^3$$
$$F_2(s) = 2779^3 + 2382^3 + 1588^3 + 794^3 = 631 \cdot 397^3$$
$$= 39482157763$$

Solution 2:

$$u = 2779, v = 2382, x = 1588, y = 794, z = 397$$

From $F_1(s)$ and $F_2(s)$ we have

$$5955^3 + (-5558)^3 = 2779^3 + 2382^3 + 1588^3 + 794^3 = 631 \cdot 397^3$$

Or

$$5955^3 + (-5558)^3 = 2779^3 + 2382^3 + 1588^3 + 794^3$$

Then

$$5558^3 + 2779^3 + 2382^3 + 1588^3 + 794^3 = 5955^3$$

Solution:

$$5558^3 + 2779^3 + 2382^3 + 1588^3 + 794^3 = 5955^3$$

---

*) Find the values of a, b, c, d, e, f of the Diophantine equation below

$$a^3 + b^3 + c^3 + d^3 + e^3 = f^3$$

Unknowns take the whole numbers

Given: the smallest value has 3 digits

Solve

Similarly, I am applying my popular method for to find the values a, b, c, d, e, f of the Diophantine equation following:

$$a^3 + b^3 + c^3 + d^3 + e^3 = f^3$$

$$\zeta(s) = r^n + s^n = c$$

$$s = {}^n\!\sqrt{c - r^n}$$
$$r = {}^n\!\sqrt{c - s^n}$$
$$\zeta(s) = c \ \& \ \zeta(c) = 0$$
$$x = r \cdot z = {}^n\!\sqrt{c - s^n} \cdot z$$
$$y = s \cdot z = {}^n\!\sqrt{c - r^n} \cdot z$$

$$n \to \infty$$

The values of r, s, t, u as following

$$\zeta_1(s) = r^n + s^n = c$$
$$\zeta_1(s) = r^3 + s^3 = 721$$
$$16^3 + (-15)^3 = 721$$

And

$$\zeta_2(s) = r^n + s^n + t^n + u^n = c$$
$$\zeta_2(s) = r^3 + s^3 + t^3 + u^3 = 721$$
$$7^3 + 7^3 + 3^3 + 2^3 = 721$$

Applying the popular method for finding the values of a, b, c, d, e and f

$$\zeta(s) = r^n + s^n = c$$

$$s = {}^n\!\sqrt{c - r^n}$$
$$r = {}^n\!\sqrt{c - s^n}$$
$$\zeta(s) = c \ \& \ \zeta(c) = 0$$
$$x = r \cdot z = {}^n\!\sqrt{c - s^n} \cdot z$$
$$y = s \cdot z = {}^n\!\sqrt{c - r^n} \cdot z$$

$$n \to \infty$$

206

Back to the Fermat-Wiles Equation below

$$F_1(s) = x^3 + y^3 = 721 \cdot z^3$$
$$F_2(s) = u^3 + v^3 + x^3 + y^3 = 721 \cdot z^3$$

The values of u, v, x, y, z
The first approach to $F_1(s)$

$$\zeta(s) = c \text{ and } \zeta(c) = 0$$

Find the values of r, s of $F_1(s)$

$$c = 721$$
$$\zeta(s)_1 = r^3 + s^3 = 721$$
$$\zeta(s)_1 = 16^3 + (-15)^3 = 721$$

$$x = r \cdot z$$
$$y = s \cdot z$$

The values of x, y
Choose any value of z (z = 401)

$$x = r \cdot z = 16 \cdot 401 = 6416$$
$$y = s \cdot z = -15 \cdot 401 = -6015$$

Replace these values into $F_1(s)$
Try again

$$F_1(s) = x^3 + y^3 = 721 \cdot z^3$$
$$F_1(s) = 6416^3 + (-6015)^3 = 721 \cdot 401^3$$
$$= 46490945921$$

Solution 1:

$$x = 6416, y = -6015, z = 401$$

The next step to Diophantine equation $F_2(s)$

Find the values of r, s, t, u of $\zeta(s)_2$ of $F_2(s)$

$$\zeta(s)_2 = r^3 + s^3 + t^3 + u^3 = 721$$
$$\zeta(s)_2 = 7^3 + 7^3 + 3^3 + 2^3 = 721$$

$$u = r \cdot z$$
$$v = s \cdot z$$
$$x = t \cdot z$$
$$y = u \cdot z$$

The values of u, v, x, y

$$z = 401$$
$$u = r \cdot z = 7 \cdot 401 = 2807$$
$$v = s \cdot z = 7v401 = 2807$$
$$x = t \cdot z = 3 \cdot 401 = 1203$$
$$y = u \cdot z = 2 \cdot 401 = 802$$

Replace these values into $F_2(s)$

Try again

$$F_2(s) = u^3 + v^3 + x^3 + y^3 = 721 \cdot z^3$$
$$F_2(s) = 2807^3 + 2807^3 + 1203^3 + 802^3 = 721 \cdot 401^3$$
$$= 46490945921$$

Solution 2:

$$u = 2807, v = 2807, x = 1203, y = 802, z = 401$$

From $F_1(s)$ and $F_2(s)$

We have

$$6416^3 + (-6015)^3 = 2807^3 + 2807^3 + 1203^3 + 802^3 = 721 \cdot 401^3$$

Or

$$6416^3 + (-6015)^3 = 2807^3 + 2807^3 + 1203^3 + 802^3$$

Then

$$6015^3 + 2807^3 + 2807^3 + 1203^3 + 802^3 = 6416^3$$

Solution:

$$6015^3 + 2807^3 + 2807^3 + 1203^3 + 802^3 = 6416^3$$

Other Diophantine equation

Ex:

$$a^3 + b^3 + c^3 = d^3 + e^3 + f^3$$

Solution

$$911^3 + 7^3 + 1^3 = 910^3 + 135^3 + 30^3$$

EXERCISES

*) Find the values of a, b, c, d, e, f of the Diophantine equation below

$$a^3 + b^3 + c^3 + d^3 + e^3 = f^3$$

Unknowns take the whole numbers

Given: the smallest value has 2 digits

*) Find the values of a, b, c, d, e, f of the Diophantine equation below

$$a^3 + b^3 + c^3 + d^3 + e^3 = f^3$$

Unknowns take the whole numbers

Given: gcd (a,b,c,d,e) = 41

*) Find the values of a, b, c, d, e, f of the Diophantine equation below

$$a^3 + b^3 + c^3 + d^3 + e^3 = f^3$$

Unknowns take the whole numbers

Given: the smallest value has 3 digits

*) Find the values of a, b, c, d, e, f of the Diophantine equation below

$$a^3 + b^3 + c^3 + d^3 + e^3 = f^3$$

Unknowns take the whole numbers

Given: gcd (a,b,c,d,e) = 411

*) Find the values of a, b, c, d, e, f of the Diophantine equation below

$$a^3 + b^3 + c^3 + d^3 + e^3 = f^3$$

Unknowns take the whole numbers

Given: the smallest value has 4 digits

*) Find the values of a, b, c, d, e, f of the Diophantine equation below

$$a^3 + b^3 + c^3 + d^3 + e^3 = f^3$$

Unknowns take the whole numbers

Given: gcd (a,b,c,d,e) = 143

*) Find the values of a, b, c, d, e, f of the Diophantine equation below

$$a^3 + b^3 + c^3 + d^3 + e^3 = f^3$$

Unknowns take the whole numbers

Given: the smallest value has 5 digits

*) Find the values of a, b, c, d, e, f of the Diophantine equation below

$$a^3 + b^3 + c^3 + d^3 + e^3 = f^3$$

Unknowns take the whole numbers

Given: gcd (a,b,c,d,e) = 741

*) Find the values of a, b, c, d, e, f of the Diophantine equation below

$$a^3 + b^3 + c^3 + d^3 + e^3 = f^3$$

Unknowns take the whole numbers

Given: the smallest value has 6 digits

*) Find the values of a, b, c, d, e, f of the Diophantine equation below

$$a^3 + b^3 + c^3 + d^3 + e^3 = f^3$$

Unknowns take the whole numbers

Given: the smallest value has 6 digits

*) Find the values of a, b, c, d, e, f of the Diophantine equation below

$$a^3 + b^3 + c^3 + d^3 + e^3 = f^3$$

Unknowns take the whole numbers

Given: the smallest value has 7 digits

*) Find the values of a, b, c, d, e, f of the Diophantine equation below

$$a^3 + b^3 + c^3 = d^3 + e^3 + f^3$$

Unknowns take the whole numbers

*) Find the values of a, b, c, d, e, f of the Diophantine equation below

$$a^3 + b^3 + c^3 = d^3 + e^3 + f^3$$

Unknowns take the whole numbers

*) Find the values of a, b, c, d, e, f of the Diophantine equation below

$$a^3 + b^3 + c^3 = d^3 + e^3 + f^3$$

Unknowns take the whole numbers

*) Find the values of a, b, c, d, e, f of the Diophantine equation below

$$a^3 + b^3 + c^3 = d^3 + e^3 + f^3$$

Unknowns take the whole numbers

*) Find the values of a, b, c, d, e, f of the Diophantine equation below

$$a^3 + b^3 + c^3 = d^3 + e^3 + f^3$$

Unknowns take the whole numbers

—————————————————

EXPAND DIOPHANTINE EQUATIONS
$A^3 + B^3 + C^3 + D^3 + E^3 + F^3 = G^3$

Expanded from 3 unknowns of the Fermat-Wiles equation to the Diophantine equation, get 7 unknowns

Example:

*) Find the values of a, b, c, d, e, f, g of the Diophantine equation below

$a^3 + b^3 + c^3 + d^3 + e^3 + f^3 = g^3$

Unknowns take the whole numbers

Given: the smallest value has 3 digits

Solve

Similarly, I am applying my popular method for to find the values a, b, c, d, e, f, g of the Diophantine equation following:

$$a^3 + b^3 + c^3 + d^3 + e^3 + f^3 = g^3$$

$$\zeta(s) = r^n + s^n = c$$

$$s = \sqrt[n]{c - r^n}$$
$$r = \sqrt[n]{c - s^n}$$
$$\zeta(s) = c \ \& \ \zeta(c) = 0$$
$$x = r \cdot z = \sqrt[n]{c - s^n \cdot z}$$
$$y = s \cdot z = \sqrt[n]{c - r^n \cdot z}$$

$$n \to \infty$$

The values of r, s, *t, u, v* as following

$$\zeta_1(s) = r^n + s^n = c$$
$$\zeta_1(s) = r^3 + s^3 = 631$$
$$15^3 + (-14)^3 = 631$$

And

$$\zeta_2(s) = r^n + s^n + t^n + u^n + v^n = c$$
$$\zeta_2(s) = r^3 + s^3 + t^3 + u^3 + v^3 = 631$$
$$8^3 + 4^3 + 3^3 + 3^3 + 1^3 = 631$$

Find the values of a, b, c, d, e, f and g

$$\zeta(s) = r^n + s^n = c$$

$$s = \sqrt[n]{c - r^n}$$
$$r = \sqrt[n]{c - s^n}$$
$$\zeta(s) = c \ \& \ \zeta(c) = 0$$
$$x = r \cdot z = \sqrt[n]{c - s^n \cdot z}$$
$$y = s \cdot z = \sqrt[n]{c - r^n \cdot z}$$

$$n \to \infty$$

Back to the Fermat-Wiles Equation below

$$F_1(s) = x^3 + y^3 = 631 \cdot z^3$$

$$F_2(s) = t^3 + u^3 + v^3 + x^3 + y^3 = 631 \cdot z^3$$

The values of t, u, v, x, y, z
The first approach to $F_1(s)$

$$\zeta(s) = c \text{ and } \zeta(c) = 0$$

Find the values of r, s of $F_1(s)$

$$c = 631$$
$$\zeta(s)_1 = r^3 + s^3 = 631$$
$$\zeta(s)_1 = 15^3 + (-14)^3 = 631$$

$$x = r \cdot z$$
$$y = s \cdot z$$

The values of x, y
Choose any value of z (z = 419)

$$x = r \cdot z = 15 \cdot 419 = 6285$$
$$y = s \cdot z = -14 \cdot 419 = -5866$$

Replace these values into $F_1(s)$
Try again

$$F_1(s) = x^3 + y^3 = 631 \cdot z^3$$
$$F_1(s) = 6285^3 + (-5866)^3 = 631 \cdot 419^3$$
$$= 46416397229$$

Solution 1:

$$x = 6285, y = -5866, z = 419$$

The next step to Diophantine equation $F_2(s)$

Find the values of r, s, t, u of $\zeta(s)_2$ of $F_2(s)$

$$\zeta(s)_2 = r^3 + s^3 + t^3 + u^3 + v^3 = 631$$
$$\zeta(s)_2 = 8^3 + 4^3 + 3^3 + 3^3 + 1^3 = 631$$

$$t = r \cdot z$$
$$u = s \cdot z$$
$$v = t \cdot z$$
$$x = u \cdot z$$
$$y = v \cdot z$$

The values of t, u, v, x, y

$$z = 419$$
$$t = r \cdot z = 8 \cdot 419 = 3352$$
$$u = s \cdot z = 4 \cdot 419 = 1676$$
$$v = t \cdot z = 3 \cdot 419 = 1257$$
$$x = u \cdot z = 3 \cdot 419 = 1257$$
$$y = v \cdot z = 1 \cdot 419 = 419$$

Replace these values into $F_2(s)$

Try again

$$F_2(s) = t^3 + u^3 + v^3 + x^3 + y^3 = 631 \cdot z^3$$
$$F_2(s) = 3352^3 + 1676^3 + 1257^3 + 1257^3 + 419^3 = 631 \cdot 419^3$$
$$= 46416397229$$

Solution 2:

$t = 3352 \; u = 1676, \; v = 1257, \; x = 1257, \; y = 419, \; z = 419$

From $F_1(s)$ and $F_2(s)$

We have

$6285^3 + (-5866)^3 = 3352^3 + 1676^3 + 1257^3 + 1257^3 + 419^3$

$= 631 \cdot 419^3$

Or

$6285^3 + (-5866)^3 = 3352^3 + 1676^3 + 1257^3 + 1257^3 + 419^3$

Then

$5866^3 + 3352^3 + 1676^3 + 1257^3 + 1257^3 + 419^3 = 6285^3$

Soluion1:

$$a^3 + b^3 + c^3 + d^3 + e^3 + f^3 = g^3$$

$5866^3 + 3352^3 + 1676^3 + 1257^3 + 1257^3 + 419^3 = 6285^3$

Soluion2:

$$a^3 + b^3 + c^3 + d^3 + e^3 + f^3 = g^3$$

$459576^3 + 67758^3 + 6874^3 + 2946^3 + 1964^3 + 491^3 = 460067^3$

---

*) Find the values of a, b, c, d, e, f, g, h of the Diophantine equation below

$$a^3 + b^3 + c^3 + d^3 + e^3 + f^3 + g^3 = h^3$$

Unknowns take the whole numbers

Given: the smallest value has 3 digits

Solve

Similarly, I am applying my popular method for to find the values a, b, c, d, e, f, g, h, of the Diophantine equation following:

$$a^3 + b^3 + c^3 + d^3 + e^3 + f^3 + g^3 = h^3$$

$$\zeta(s) = r^n + s^n = c$$

$$s = \sqrt[n]{c - r^n}$$
$$r = \sqrt[n]{c - s^n}$$
$$\zeta(s) = c \ \& \ \zeta(c) = 0$$
$$x = r \cdot z = \sqrt[n]{c - s^n \cdot z}$$
$$y = s \cdot z = \sqrt[n]{c - r^n \cdot z}$$

$$n \to \infty$$

The values of r, s, *t, u, v, x* as following

$$\zeta_1(s) = r^n + s^n = c$$
$$\zeta_1(s) = r^3 + s^3 = 1647$$
$$15^3 + (-12)^3 = 1647$$

And

$$\zeta_2(s) = r^n + s^n + t^n + u^n + v^n + x^n = c$$
$$\zeta_2(s) = r^3 + s^3 + t^3 + u^3 + v^3 + x^3 = 1647$$
$$11^3 + 6^3 + 4^3 + 3^3 + 2^3 + 1^3 = 1647$$

The next step we use the popular method for to find the values of a, b, c, d, e f, g and h

$$\zeta(s) = r^n + s^n = c$$

$$s = \sqrt[n]{c - r^n}$$

$$r = \sqrt[n]{c - s^n}$$

$$\zeta(s) = c \,\&\, \zeta(c) = 0$$

$$x = r \cdot z = \sqrt[n]{c - s^n \cdot z}$$

$$y = s \cdot z = \sqrt[n]{c - r^n \cdot z}$$

$$n \to \infty$$

Back to the Fermat-Wiles Equation below

$$F_1(s) = x^3 + y^3 = 1647 \cdot z^3$$

$$F_2(s) = s^3 + t^3 + u^3 + v^3 + x^3 + y^3 = 1647 \cdot z^3$$

The values of s, t, u, v, x, y, z

The first approach to $F_1(s)$

$$\zeta(s) = c \text{ and } \zeta(c) = 0$$

Find the values of r, s of $F_1(s)$

$$c = 1647$$

$$\zeta(s)_1 = r^3 + s^3 = 1647$$

$$\zeta(s)_1 = 15^3 + (-12)^3 = 1647$$

$$x = r \cdot z$$

$$y = s \cdot z$$

The values of x, y

Choose any value of z (z = 431)

$$x = r \cdot z = 15 \cdot 431 = 6465$$
$$y = s \cdot z = -12 \cdot 431 = -5172$$

Replace these values into $F_1(s)$

Try again

$$F_1(s) = x^3 + y^3 = 1647 \cdot z^3$$
$$F_1(s) = 6465^3 + (-5172)^3 = 1647 \cdot 431^3$$
$$= 131863746177$$

Solution 1:

$$x = 6465, y = -5172, z = 431$$

The next step to Diophantine equation $F_2(s)$

Find the values of r, s, t, u, v, x of $\zeta(s)_2$ of $F_2(s)$

$$\zeta(s)_2 = r^3 + s^3 + t^3 + u^3 + v^3 + x^3 = 1647$$
$$\zeta(s)_2 = 11^3 + 6^3 + 4^3 + 3^3 + 2^3 + 1^3 = 1647$$

Then

$$s = r \cdot z$$
$$t = s \cdot z$$
$$u = t \cdot z$$
$$v = u \cdot z$$
$$x = v \cdot z$$
$$y = x \cdot z$$

The values of s, t, u, v, x, y

$$z = 431$$
$$s = r \cdot z = 11 \cdot 431 = 4741$$
$$t = s \cdot z = 6 \cdot 431 = 2586$$
$$u = t \cdot z = 4 \cdot 431 = 1724$$
$$v = u \cdot z = 3 \cdot 431 = 1293$$
$$x = v \cdot z = 2 \cdot 431 = 862$$
$$y = x \cdot z = 1 \cdot 431 = 431$$

Replace these values into $F_2(s)$

Try again

$$F_2(s) = s^3 + t^3 + u^3 + v^3 + x^3 + y^3 = 631 \cdot z^3$$
$$F_2(s) = 4741^3 + 2586^3 + 1724^3 + 1293^3 + 862^3 + 431^3 = 1647 \cdot 431^3$$
$$= 131863746177$$

Solution 2:

s = 4741, t = 2586 u = 1724, v = 1293, x = 862, y = 431, z = 431

From $F_1(s)$ and $F_2(s)$

We have

$$6465^3 + (-5172)^3 = 4741^3 + 2586^3 + 1724^3 + 1293^3 + 862^3 + 431^3$$
$$= 1647 \cdot 431^3$$

Or

$$6465^3 + (-5172)^3 = 4741^3 + 2586^3 + 1724^3 + 1293^3 + 862^3 + 431^3$$

Then

$$5172^3 + 4741^3 + 2586^3 + 1724^3 + 1293^3 + 862^3 + 431^3 = 6465^3$$

Soluion:

$$a^3 + b^3 + c^3 + d^3 + e^3 + f^3 + g^3 = h^3$$

$$5172^3 + 4741^3 + 2586^3 + 1724^3 + 1293^3 + 862^3 + 431^3 = 6465^3$$

EXERCISES

*) Find the values of a, b, c, d, e, f, g of the Diophantine equation below

$$a^3 + b^3 + c^3 + d^3 + e^3 + f^3 = g^3$$

Unknowns take the whole numbers

Given: the smallest value has 2 digits

*) Find the values of a, b, c, d, e, f, g of the Diophantine equation below

$$a^3 + b^3 + c^3 + d^3 + e^3 + f^3 = g^3$$

Unknowns take the whole numbers

Given: the smallest value has 2 digits

*) Find the values of a, b, c, d, e, f, g of the Diophantine equation below

$$a^3 + b^3 + c^3 + d^3 + e^3 + f^3 = g^3$$

Unknowns take the whole numbers

Given: the smallest value has 3 digits

*) Find the values of a, b, c, d, e, f, g of the Diophantine equation below

$$a^3 + b^3 + c^3 + d^3 + e^3 + f^3 = g^3$$

Unknowns take the whole numbers

Given: the smallest value has 3 digits

*) Find the values of a, b, c, d, e, f, g of the Diophantine equation below

$$a^3 + b^3 + c^3 + d^3 + e^3 + f^3 = g^3$$

Unknowns take the whole numbers

Given: the smallest value has 4 digits

*) Find the values of a, b, c, d, e, f, g of the Diophantine equation below

$$a^3 + b^3 + c^3 + d^3 + e^3 + f^3 = g^3$$

Unknowns take the whole numbers

Given: the smallest value has 4 digits

*) Find the values of a, b, c, d, e, f, g of the Diophantine equation below

$$a^3 + b^3 + c^3 + d^3 + e^3 + f^3 = g^3$$

Unknowns take the whole numbers

Given: the smallest value has 5 digits

*) Find the values of a, b, c, d, e, f, g of the Diophantine equation below

$$a^3 + b^3 + c^3 + d^3 + e^3 + f^3 = g^3$$

Unknowns take the whole numbers

Given: the smallest value has 5 digits

*) Find the values of a, b, c, d, e, f, g of the Diophantine equation below

$$a^3 + b^3 + c^3 + d^3 + e^3 + f^3 = g^3$$

Unknowns take the whole numbers

Given: the smallest value has 6 digits

*) Find the values of a, b, c, d, e, f, g of the Diophantine equation below

$$a^3 + b^3 + c^3 + d^3 + e^3 + f^3 = g^3$$

Unknowns take the whole numbers

Given: the smallest value has 7 digits

*) Find the values of a, b, c, d, e, f, g of the Diophantine equation below

$$a^3 + b^3 + c^3 + d^3 + e^3 + f^3 = g^3$$

Unknowns take the whole numbers

Given: the smallest value has 8 digits

*) Find the values of a, b, c, d, e, f, g, h of the Diophantine equation below

$$a^3 + b^3 + c^3 + d^3 + e^3 + f^3 + g^3 = h^3$$

Unknowns take the whole numbers

Given: the smallest value has 2 digits

*) Find the values of a, b, c, d, e, f, g, h of the Diophantine equation below

$$a^3 + b^3 + c^3 + d^3 + e^3 + f^3 + g^3 = h^3$$

Unknowns take the whole numbers

Given: the smallest value has 3 digits

*) Find the values of a, b, c, d, e, f, g, h of the Diophantine equation below

$$a^3 + b^3 + c^3 + d^3 + e^3 + f^3 + g^3 = h^3$$

Unknowns take the whole numbers

Given: the smallest value has 4 digits

*) Find the values of a, b, c, d, e, f, g, h of the Diophantine equation below

$$a^3 + b^3 + c^3 + d^3 + e^3 + f^3 + g^3 = h^3$$

Unknowns take the whole numbers

Given: the smallest value has 5 digits

*) Find the values of a, b, c, d, e, f, g, h of the Diophantine equation below

$$a^3 + b^3 + c^3 + d^3 + e^3 + f^3 + g^3 = h^3$$

Unknowns take the whole numbers

Given: the smallest value has 6 digits

*) Find the values of a, b, c, d, e, f, g, h, i of the Diophantine equation below

$$a^3 + b^3 + c^3 + d^3 + e^3 + f^3 + g^3 + h^3 = i^3$$

Unknowns take the whole numbers

Given: the smallest value has 3 digits

*) Find the values of a, b, c, d, e, f, g, h, i of the Diophantine equation below

$$a^3 + b^3 + c^3 + d^3 + e^3 + f^3 + g^3 + h^3 = i^3$$

Unknowns take the whole numbers

Given: the smallest value has 4 digits

FERMAT-WILES EQUATION
$x^n + y^n = c \cdot z^n \quad n = 4$

$$x^4 + y^4 = c \cdot z^4$$

Similar above, we find the value of c

Applying the popular method

$$\zeta(s) = r^n + s^n = c$$

$$s = \sqrt[n]{c - r^n}$$
$$r = \sqrt[n]{c - s^n}$$
$$\zeta(s) = c \ \& \ \zeta(c) = 0$$
$$x = r \cdot z = \sqrt[n]{c - s^n} \cdot z$$
$$y = s \cdot z = \sqrt[n]{c - r^n} \cdot z$$

$$n \to \infty$$

I find the value of c by the popular methods, with n = 4

r^4	s^4	c		2^4	3^4	97
1^4	1^4	2		3^4	3^4	162
1^4	2^4	17		4^4	1^4	257
2^4	2^4	32		4^4	2^4	272
1^4	3^4	82		4^4	3^4	337

4^4	4^4	512	8^4	2^4	4112
5^4	1^4	626	8^4	3^4	4177
5^4	2^4	641	8^4	4^4	4352
5^4	3^4	706	8^4	5^4	4721
r^4	s^4	c	8^4	6^4	5392
5^4	4^4	881	8^4	7^4	6497
5^4	5^4	1250	8^4	8^4	8192
6^4	1^4	1297	9^4	1^4	6562
6^4	2^4	1312	9^4	2^4	6577
6^4	3^4	1377	9^4	3^4	6642
6^4	4^4	1552	9^4	4^4	6817
6^4	5^4	1921	9^4	5^4	7186
6^4	6^4	2592	9^4	6^4	7857
7^4	1^4	2402	9^4	7^4	8962
7^4	2^4	2417	9^4	8^4	10657
7^4	3^4	2482	9^4	9^4	13122
7^4	4^4	2657	10^4	1^4	10001
7^4	5^4	3026	10^4	2^4	10016
7^4	6^4	3697	10^4	3^4	10081
7^4	7^4	4802			
8^4	1^4	4097			

….

On internet we see

The table of values of c by the mathematician "Bremner and Morton"

"2, 17, 32, 82, 97, 162, 257, 272, 337, 512, 626, 641, 706, 881, 1250, 1297, 1312, 1377, 1552, 1921, 2402, 2417, 2482, 2592, 2657, 3026, 3697, 4097, 4112, 4177, 4352, 4721, 4802, 5392, 5906, ... and that 5906 = (149/17)⁴ + (25/17)⁴"

5906, ... and that $5906 = (149/17)^4 + (25/17)^4$"

APPLICATION

*) Find the values of x, y, z of the Fermat- Wiles Equation below

$$x^4 + y^4 = 97 \cdot z^4$$

Unknowns take the whole numbers

Solve

Fermat- Wiles Equation:

$$x^4 + y^4 = 97 \cdot z^4$$

Applying the popular method

$$\zeta(s) = r^n + s^n = c$$

$$s = \sqrt[n]{c - r^n}$$
$$r = \sqrt[n]{c - s^n}$$
$$\zeta(s) = c \ \& \ \zeta(c) = 0$$
$$x = r \cdot z = \sqrt[n]{c - s^n \cdot z}$$
$$y = s \cdot z = \sqrt[n]{c - r^n \cdot z}$$

$$n \rightarrow \infty$$

Find the values of r, s

$$c = 97$$
$$\zeta(s) = r^4 + s^4 = 97$$
$$\zeta(s) = 2^4 + 3^4 = 97$$

The values of x, y, z

$$x = r \cdot z$$
$$y = s \cdot z$$

The value of z

Choose any value of z (i.e., 1, 2, 3, 4, 5, 6, 7,…)

$$z = 4$$

The value of x

$$x = r \cdot z$$
$$x = 2 \cdot 4 = 8$$

The value of y

$$y = s \cdot z$$
$$y = 3 \cdot 4 = 12$$

Replace these values into the Diophantine equation

Try again

$$x^4 + y^4 = 97 \cdot z^4$$
$$8^4 + 12^4 = 97 \cdot 4^4 = 24832$$

Solution: x = 8, y = 12, z = 4

---

*) Find the values of x, y, z of the Fermat- Wiles Equation below

$$x^4 + y^4 = 337 \cdot z^4$$

Unknowns take the whole numbers

Solve

Fermat- Wiles Equation:

$$x^4 + y^4 = 337 \cdot z^4$$

Applying the popular method

$$\zeta(s) = r^n + s^n = c$$

$$s = \sqrt[n]{c - r^n}$$
$$r = \sqrt[n]{c - s^n}$$
$$\zeta(s) = c \ \& \ \zeta(c) = 0$$
$$x = r \cdot z = \sqrt[n]{c - s^n \cdot z}$$
$$y = s \cdot z = \sqrt[n]{c - r^n \cdot z}$$

$$n \rightarrow \infty$$

Find the values of r, s

$$c = 337$$
$$\zeta(s) = r^4 + s^4 = 337$$
$$\zeta(s) = 4^4 + 3^4 = 337$$

The values of x, y, z

$$x = r \cdot z$$
$$y = s \cdot z$$

The value of z

Choose any value of z (i.e., 1, 2, 3, 4, 5, 6, 7,...)

$$z = 7$$

The value of x

$$x = r \cdot z$$
$$x = 4 \cdot 7 = 28$$

The value of y

$$y = s \cdot z$$
$$y = 3 \cdot 7 = 21$$

Replace these values into the Diophantine equation

Try again

$$x^4 + y^4 = 337 \cdot z^4$$
$$28^4 + 21^4 = 337 \cdot 7^4 = 809137$$

Solution: x = 28, y = 21, z = 7

_____

*) Find the values of x, y, z of the Fermat- Wiles Equation below

$$x^4 + y^4 = 706 \cdot z^4$$

Unknowns take the whole numbers

Solve

Fermat- Wiles Equation:

$$x^4 + y^4 = 706 \cdot z^4$$

Applying the popular method

$$\zeta(s) = r^n + s^n = c$$

$$s = \sqrt[n]{c - r^n}$$
$$r = \sqrt[n]{c - s^n}$$
$$\zeta(s) = c \ \& \ \zeta(c) = 0$$
$$x = r \cdot z = \sqrt[n]{c - s^n \cdot z}$$
$$y = s \cdot z = \sqrt[n]{c - r^n \cdot z}$$

$$n \to \infty$$

Find the values of r, s

$$c = 706$$
$$\zeta(s) = r^4 + s^4 = 706$$
$$\zeta(s) = 5^4 + 3^4 = 706$$

The values of x, y, z

$$x = r \cdot z$$
$$y = s \cdot z$$

The value of z

Choose any value of z (i.e., 1, 2, 3, 4, 5, 6, 7,...)

$$z = 6$$

The value of x
$$x = r \cdot z$$
$$x = 5 \cdot 6 = 30$$
The value of y
$$y = s \cdot z$$
$$y = 3 \cdot 6 = 18$$

Replace these values into the Diophantine equation
Try again
$$x^4 + y^4 = 706 \cdot z^4$$
$$30^4 + 18^4 = 706 \cdot 6^4 = 914976$$

Solution: x = 30, y = 18, z = 6

...

———————————

*) There are many candies in candy box, with three different colors, green, yellow and purple. If the 4th powers of the green, and yellow candies, then sum of both, it's equal to multiple of 641 by the 4th power of purple candies

Given: 19 purple candies
How many candies of each color?

Solve

We put

> A= green candies
>
> B = yellow candies
>
> C = purple candies

We have

$$F_1(s) = A^4 + B^4 = 641 \cdot C^4$$

Back to problem Fermat - Wiles equaion

$$x^n + y^n = c \cdot z^n$$

Applying the popular method with n = 4

$$\zeta(s) = r^n + s^n = c$$

$$s = \sqrt[n]{c - r^n}$$
$$r = \sqrt[n]{c - s^n}$$
$$\zeta(s) = c \ \& \ \zeta(c) = 0$$
$$x = r \cdot z = \sqrt[n]{c - s^n} \cdot z$$
$$y = s \cdot z = \sqrt[n]{c - r^n} \cdot z$$

$$n \to \infty$$

The values of A, B, C

$$\zeta(s) = c \text{ and } \zeta(c) = 0$$

Find the values of r, s

$$c = 641$$
$$\zeta(s) = r^4 + s^4 = 641$$
$$\zeta(s)_1 = 5^4 + 2^4 = 641$$

The values of A, B

$$\zeta(s) = 5^4 + 2^4 = 641$$
$$A = 5 \cdot C$$
$$B = 2 \cdot C$$

The values of A, B

$$C = 19 \text{ candies}$$
$$A = 5 \cdot C = 5 \cdot 19 = 95 \text{ candies}$$
$$B = 2 \cdot C = 2 \cdot 19 = 38 \text{ candies}$$

Replace these values in F1 (s) to try again

$$F_1(s) = A^4 + B^4 = 641 \cdot C^4$$
$$= 95^4 + 38^4 = 641 \cdot 19^4 = 83535761$$

Solution 1:

A = green candies: 95
B = yellow candies 38
C = purple candies 19

————————————

*) There are many candies in candy box, with three different colors, green, yellow and purple. If the 4th powers of the

green, and yellow candies, then sum of both, it's equal to the 5th power of purple candies

Given: 6817 purple candies

How many candies of green and yellow?

Solve

We put

A= green candies

B = yellow candies

C = purple candies

We have

$$F_1(s) = A^4 + B^4 = C^5$$

We rewrite $F_1(s)$ to $F_2(s)$

$$F_2(s) = A^4 + B^4 = C \cdot C^4$$

Back to problem Fermat-Wiles equaion

$$x^n + y^n = c \cdot z^n$$

Applying the popular method with n = 4

$$\zeta(s) = r^n + s^n = c$$

$$s = \sqrt[n]{c - r^n}$$
$$r = \sqrt[n]{c - s^n}$$

$$\zeta(s) = c \ \& \ \zeta(c) = 0$$
$$x = r \cdot z = \sqrt[n]{c - s^n \cdot z}$$
$$y = s \cdot z = \sqrt[n]{c - r^n \cdot z}$$
$$n \to \infty$$

The values of A, B, C

$$\zeta(s) = c \text{ and } \zeta(c) = 0$$

Replace C by c

Find the values of r, s

$$c = 6817$$
$$\zeta(s) = r^4 + s^4 = 6817$$
$$\zeta(s)_1 = 4^4 + 9^4 = 6817$$

The values of A, B

$$\zeta(s) = 4^4 + 9^4 = 6817$$
$$A = r \cdot C$$
$$B = s \cdot C$$

The values of A, B

$$C = 6817 \text{ candies}$$
$$A = r \cdot C = 4 \cdot 6817 = 27268 \text{ candies}$$
$$B = s \cdot C = 9 \cdot 6817 = 61353 \text{ candies}$$

Replace these values into $F_1(s)$
Try again

$$F_1(s) = A^4 + B^4 = C^5$$
$$F_1(s) = 27268^4 + 61353^4 = 6817^5 = 14721988359092333857$$

Solution:

A = green candies: 27268

B = yellow candies 61353

C = purple candies 6817

EXERCISES

*) Find the values of x, y, z of the Fermat- Wiles Equation below

$$x^4 + y^4 = 626 \cdot z^4$$

Unknowns take the whole numbers

*) Find the values of x, y, z of the Fermat- Wiles Equation below

$$x^4 + y^4 = 881 \cdot z^4$$

Unknowns take the whole numbers

*) Find the values of x, y, z of the Fermat- Wiles Equation below

$$x^4 + y^4 = 1250 \cdot z^4$$

Unknowns take the whole numbers

*) Find the values of x, y, z of the Fermat- Wiles Equation below

$$x^4 + y^4 = 1297 \cdot z^4$$

Unknowns take the whole numbers

*) Find the values of x, y, z of the Fermat- Wiles Equation below

$$x^4 + y^4 = 1312 \cdot z^4$$

Unknowns take the whole numbers

*) Find the values of x, y, z of the Fermat- Wiles Equation below

$$x^4 + y^4 = 1377 \cdot z^4$$

Unknowns take the whole numbers

*) Find the values of x, y, z of the Fermat- Wiles Equation below

$$x^4 + y^4 = 1552 \cdot z^4$$

Unknowns take the whole numbers

*) There are many candies in candy box, with three different colors, green, yellow and purple. If the 4th powers of the green, and yellow candies, then sum of both, it's equal to the 5th power of purple candies

Given: 1921 purple candies
How many candies of green and yellow?

*) There are many candies in candy box, with three different colors, green, yellow and purple. If the 4th powers of the green, and yellow candies, then sum of both, it's equal to the 5th power of purple candies

Given: 2402 purple candies
How many candies of green and yellow?

*) There are many candies in candy box, with three different colors, green, yellow and purple. If the 4th powers of the green, and yellow candies, then sum of both, it's equal to the 5th power of purple candies

Given: 2417 purple candies
How many candies of green and yellow?

*) There are many candies in candy box, with three different colors, green, yellow and purple. If the 4th powers of the green, and yellow candies, then sum of both, it's equal to the 5th power of purple candies

Given: 2482 purple candies
How many candies of green and yellow?

EXPAND DIOPHANTINE EQUATIONS
$a^4 + b^4 + c^4 + d^4 + e^4 + f^4 = g^4$

Expanded from 3 unknowns of the Fermat-Wiles equation to the Diophantine equation with 7 unknowns

Example:

*) Find the values of a, b, c, d, e, f, g of the Diophantine equation below

$$a^4 + b^4 + c^4 + d^4 + e^4 + f^4 = g^4$$

Unknowns take the whole numbers

Given: the smallest value get 3 digits

Solve

Similarly, I am applying my popular method for to find the values a, b, c, d, e, f, g, of the Diophantine equation following:

$$a^4 + b^4 + c^4 + d^4 + e^4 + f^4 = g^4$$

$$\zeta(s) = r^n + s^n = c$$

$$s = \sqrt[n]{c - r^n}$$
$$r = \sqrt[n]{c - s^n}$$
$$\zeta(s) = c \ \& \ \zeta(c) = 0$$
$$x = r \cdot z = \sqrt[n]{c - s^n \cdot z}$$
$$y = s \cdot z = \sqrt[n]{c - r^n \cdot z}$$

$$n \to \infty$$

The values of r, s, t, as following

$$\zeta_1(s) = r^n + s^n + t^n = c$$
$$\zeta_1(s) = r^4 + s^4 + t^4 = 20738$$
$$12^4 + 1^4 + 1^4 = 20738$$

And

$$\zeta_2(s) = r^n + s^n + t^n + u^n = c$$
$$\zeta_2(s) = r^4 + s^4 + t^4 + u^4 = 20738$$
$$10^4 + 9^4 + 8^4 + 3^4 = 20738$$

The next step

Applying the popular method for finding the values of a, b, c, d, e, f and g

$$\zeta(s) = r^n + s^n = c$$

$$s = \sqrt[n]{c - r^n}$$
$$r = \sqrt[n]{c - s^n}$$
$$\zeta(s) = c \ \& \ \zeta(c) = 0$$
$$x = r \cdot z = \sqrt[n]{c - s^n \cdot z}$$
$$y = s \cdot z = \sqrt[n]{c - r^n \cdot z}$$

$$n \to \infty$$

Back to the Fermat-Wiles Equation below

$$F_1(s) = v^4 + x^4 + y^4 = 20738 \cdot z^4$$
$$F_2(s) = u^4 + v^4 + x^4 + y^4 = 20738 \cdot z^4$$

The values of u, v, x, y, z

The first approach to $F_1(s)$

$$\zeta(s) = c \text{ and } \zeta(c) = 0$$

Find the values of r, s, t of $F_1(s)$

$$c = 20738$$
$$\zeta(s)_1 = r^3 + s^3 + t^3 = 20738$$
$$\zeta(s)_1 = 12^4 + 1^4 + 1^4 = 20738$$

$$v = r \cdot z$$
$$x = s \cdot z$$
$$y = t \cdot z$$

The values of v, x, y

Choose any value of z (z = 173)

$$v = r \cdot z = 12 \cdot 173 = 2076$$
$$x = s \cdot z = 1 \cdot 173 = 173$$
$$y = t \cdot z = 1 \cdot 173 = 173$$

Replace these values into $F_1(s)$

Try again

$$F_1(s) = v^4 + x^4 + y^4 = 20738 \cdot z^4$$
$$F_1(s) = 2076^4 + 173^4 + 173^4 = 20738 \cdot 173^4$$
$$= 18575960660258$$

Solution 1:

$$v = 2076, x = 173, y = 173, z = 173$$

The next step to Diophantine equation $F_2(s)$

Find the values of r, s, t, u of $\zeta(s)_2$ of $F_2(s)$

$$\zeta(s)_2 = r^4 + s^4 + t^4 + u^4 = 20738$$
$$\zeta(s)_2 = 10^4 + 9^4 + 8^4 + 3^4 = 20738$$

Then

$$u = r \cdot z$$
$$v = s \cdot z$$
$$x = t \cdot z$$
$$y = u \cdot z$$

The values of u, v, x, y

$$z = 173$$
$$u = r \cdot z = 10 \cdot 173 = 1730$$
$$v = s \cdot z = 9 \cdot 173 = 1557$$
$$x = t \cdot z = 8 \cdot 173 = 1384$$
$$y = u \cdot z = 3 \cdot 173 = 519$$

Replace these values into $F_2(s)$

Try again

$$F_2(s) = u^4 + v^4 + x^4 + y^4 = 20738 \cdot z^4$$
$$F_2(s) = 1730^4 + 1557^4 + 1384^4 + 519^4 = 20738 \cdot 173^4$$
$$= 18575960660258$$

Solution 2:

u = 1730, v = 1557, x = 1384, y = 519, z = 173

From $F_1(s)$ and $F_2(s)$

We have

$$2076^4 + 173^4 + 173^4 = 1730^4 + 1557^4 + 1384^4 + 519^4$$
$$= 20738 \cdot 173^4$$

Or

$$2076^4 + 173^4 + 173^4 = 1730^4 + 1557^4 + 1384^4 + 519^4$$

Then

$$1730^4 + 1557^4 + 1384^4 + 519^4 - 173^4 - 173^4 = 2076^4$$

Soluion:

$$a^4 + b^4 + c^4 + d^4 + e^4 + f^4 = g^4$$

$$1730^4 + 1557^4 + 1384^4 + 519^4 - 173^4 - 173^4 = 2076^4$$

---

*) Find the values of a, b, c, d, e, f, g of the Diophantine equation below

$$a^4 + b^4 + c^4 + d^4 + e^4 + f^4 + g^4 = h^4$$

Unknowns take the whole numbers

Given: the smallest value get 5 digits (i.e., 10259)

Solve

Similarly, I am applying my popular method for to find the values a, b, c, d, e, f, g, h of the Diophantine equation following:

$$a^4 + b^4 + c^4 + d^4 + e^4 + f^4 + g^4 = h^4$$

$$\zeta(s) = r^n + s^n = c$$
$$s = \sqrt[n]{c - r^n}$$
$$r = \sqrt[n]{c - s^n}$$
$$\zeta(s) = c \ \& \ \zeta(c) = 0$$
$$x = r \cdot z = \sqrt[n]{c - s^n \cdot z}$$
$$y = s \cdot z = \sqrt[n]{c - r^n \cdot z}$$
$$n \to \infty$$

The values of r, s, t, as following

$$\zeta_1(s) = r^n - s^n = c$$
$$\zeta_1(s) = r^4 - s^4 = 4641$$
$$11^4 - 10^4 = 4641$$

And

$$\zeta_2(s) = r^n + s^n + t^n + u^n + v^n + x^n = c$$
$$\zeta_2(s) = r^4 + s^4 + t^4 + u^4 + v^4 + x^4 = 4641$$
$$8^4 + 4^4 + 4^4 + 2^4 + 2^4 + 1^4 = 4641$$

The next step

Applying the popular method

Find the values of a, b, c, d, e, f, g, h

We get

Solution

$$a^4 + b^4 + c^4 + d^4 + e^4 + f^4 + g^4 = h^4$$

$102590^4 + 82072^4 + 41036^4 + 41036^4 + 20518^4 + 20518^4 + 10259^4$

$= 112849^4$

Also the equation expand to thousands or more unknowns

Symbol: (n,k,1), (n,k,2), (n,k,3) ....

Example:

$$a^4 + b^4 + c^4 + d^4 + e^4 + f^4 + g^4 = h^4$$

We write (4,7,1)

$1730^4 + 1557^4 + 1384^4 + 519^4 = 2076^4 + 173^4 + 173^4$

We write (4,4,3)

*) Find the values of the unknowns of the Diophantine equation

(21, 109.418.989.131.512.359.209, 1) with n = 21 and

k = 109418989131512359209 unknowns or terms

Unknowns take the whole numbers

Similarly, I am applying my popular method for to find the values of the Diophantine equation following:

$$721^{20} \sum_{n=21}^{k=729^7} 721 = 6489^{21}$$

Try again

Left the group of the equation

$$721^{20} \sum_{n=21}^{k=729^7} 721 =$$

1.1369287723107068569046233652857e+80

Right the group of the equation

$$6489^{21} = 1.1369287723107068569046233652857e+80$$

Then

Solution of the Diophantine equation

(21, 109.418.989.131.512.359.209,1)

$$721^{20} \sum_{n=21}^{k=729^7} 721 = 6489^{21}$$

This Diophantine equation is too long, though large k, we test the length of the Diophantine equation (21, 109.418.989.131.512.359.209,1).

The length of a number of groups including the symbol + "721^{21} +" is equal to 12 ^{mm}
The length of the equation will be
1^{mm} x109.418.989.131.512.359.209 x 12
= 1.313.027.869.578.148.310.508 ^{mm}
= 1.313.027.869.578.148^{km}.

It is comparable to speed of light (c = 299 792 458 m/s)
= 4379789532. seconds
= 1216608. Hours = 50692 days = 138.88219 years
Now light years = 138.8822

The length of the Diophantine equation:
(21, 109.418.989.131.512.359.209,1) is equal to 138.2/3 light years

————————————————

EXERCISES

*) Find the values of the unknowns of the Diophantine equation

(3, 10, 1)

Unknowns take the whole numbers

*) Find the values of the unknowns of the Diophantine equation

(3, 10, 2)

Unknowns take the whole numbers

*) Find the values of the unknowns of the Diophantine equation

(3, 10, 3)

Unknowns take the whole numbers

*) Find the values of the unknowns of the Diophantine equation

(4, 12, 1)

Unknowns take the whole numbers

*) Find the values of the unknowns of the Diophantine equation

(4, 11, 2)

Unknowns take the whole numbers

*) Find the values of the unknowns of the Diophantine equation

(4, 15, 3)

*) Find the values of the unknowns of the Diophantine equation

(4, 15, 1)

Unknowns take the whole numbers

*) Find the values of the unknowns of the Diophantine equation

(4, 13, 2)

Unknowns take the whole numbers

*) Find the values of the unknowns of the Diophantine equation

(4, 14, 4)

Unknowns take the whole numbers

*) Find the values of the unknowns of the Diophantine equation

(4, 15, 1)

Unknowns take the whole numbers

*) Find the values of the unknowns of the Diophantine equation

(4, 15, 1)

Unknowns take the whole numbers

FERMAT-WILES EQUATION
$x^n + y^n = c \cdot z^n$ n = 5

$$x^5 + y^5 = c \cdot z^5$$

Similar above

Find the value of c, by the popular method below

$$\zeta(s) = r^n + s^n = c$$

$$s = \sqrt[n]{c - r^n}$$
$$r = \sqrt[n]{c - s^n}$$
$$\zeta(s) = c \ \& \ \zeta(c) = 0$$
$$x = r \cdot z = \sqrt[n]{c - s^n \cdot z}$$
$$y = s \cdot z = \sqrt[n]{c - r^n \cdot z}$$

$$n \to \infty$$

The values of c with n = 5

r5 + s5 = c	(-2)5 + 35 = 211
15 + 15 = 2	(-1)5 + 35 = 242
(-)15 + 25 = 31	15 + 35 = 244
15 + 25 = 33	25 + 35 = 275
25 + 25 = 64	35 + 35 = 486

45 + (-3)5 = 781

45 + (-2)5 = 992

45 + (-1)5 = 1023

45 + 15 = 1025

45 + 25 = 1056

45 + 35 = 1267

45 + 45 = 2048

55 + (-4)5 = 2101

55 + (-3)5 = 2882

55 + (-2)5 = 3093

55 + (-1)5 = 3124

55 + 15 = 3126

55 + 25 = 3157

55 + 35 = 3368

55 + 45 = 4149

65 + (-5)5 = 4651

55 + 55 = 6250

65 + (-4)5 = 6752

65 + (-3)5 = 7533

65 + (-2)5 = 7744

95 + (-1)5 = 59048

95 + 15 = 59050

95 + 25 = 59081

95 + 35 = 59292

95 + 45 = 60073

…

On the internet we see

The table of c values (n = 5) of mathematician David Wilson following:

"David Wilson has suggested that the c-sequence for n = 5 is:

2, 31, 33, 64, 211, 242, 244, 275, 486, 781, 992, 1023, 1025, 1056, 1267, 2048, 2101, 2882, 3093, 3124, 3126, 3157, 3368, 4149, 4651, 6250, 6752, 7533, 7744, 7775, 7777, 7808, 8019, 8800, 9031, 10901, 13682, 15552, 15783, 15961, 16564, 16775, 16806, 16808, 16839, 17050, 17831, 19932, 24583, 24992, 26281, 29643, 31744, 32525, 32736, 32767, 32769, 32800,

33011, 33614, 33792, 35893, 40544, 40951, 42242, 49575, 51273, 55924, 58025, 58806, 59017, 59048, 59050, 59081, 59292, 60073, 61051, 62174, 65536, 66825, 67232, 68101, ... and that 68101 = (15/2)⁵ + (17/2)⁵ is the least integer expressible as the sum of two rational fifth powers but not as the sum of two integer fifth powers"

---

*) Find the values of x, y, z of the Fermat- Wiles Equation below

$$x^5 + y^5 = 275 \cdot z^5$$

Unknowns take the whole numbers

Solve

Fermat- Wiles Equation:

$$x^5 + y^5 = 275 \cdot z^5$$

Applying the popular method

$$\zeta(s) = r^n + s^n = c$$

$$s = \sqrt[n]{c - r^n}$$
$$r = \sqrt[n]{c - s^n}$$
$$\zeta(s) = c \ \& \ \zeta(c) = 0$$
$$x = r \cdot z = \sqrt[n]{c - s^n \cdot z}$$
$$y = s \cdot z = \sqrt[n]{c - r^n \cdot z}$$

$$n \to \infty$$

Find the values of r, s

$$c = 275$$
$$\zeta(s) = r^5 + s^5 = 275$$
$$\zeta(s) = 2^5 + 3^5 = 275$$

The values of x, y, z

$$x = r \cdot z$$
$$y = s \cdot z$$

The value of z

Choose any value of z (i.e., 1, 2, 3, 4, 5, 6, 7,...)

$$z = 7$$

The value of x

$$x = r \cdot z$$
$$x = 2 \cdot 7 = 14$$

The value of y

$$y = s \cdot z$$
$$y = 3 \cdot 7 = 21$$

Replace these values into the Diophantine equation

Try again

$$x^5 + y^5 = 275 \cdot z^5$$
$$14^5 + 21^5 = 275 \cdot 7^5 = 4621925$$

Solution: x = 14, y = 21, z = 7

*) Find the values of x, y, z of the Fermat- Wiles Equation below

$$x^5 + y^5 = 1056 \cdot z^5$$

Unknowns take the whole numbers

Solve

Fermat- Wiles Equation:

$$x^5 + y^5 = 1056 \cdot z^5$$

Applying the popular method

$$\zeta(s) = r^n + s^n = c$$

$$s = \sqrt[n]{c - r^n}$$
$$r = \sqrt[n]{c - s^n}$$
$$\zeta(s) = c \ \& \ \zeta(c) = 0$$
$$x = r \cdot z = \sqrt[n]{c - s^n} \cdot z$$
$$y = s \cdot z = \sqrt[n]{c - r^n} \cdot z$$

$$n \to \infty$$

Find the values of r, s

$$c = 1056$$
$$\zeta(s) = r^5 + s^5 = 1056$$
$$\zeta(s) = 4^5 + 2^5 = 1056$$

The values of x, y, z

$$x = r \cdot z$$
$$y = s \cdot z$$

The value of z

Choose any value of z (i.e., 1, 2, 3, 4, 5, 6, 7,...)

$$z = 3$$

The value of x

$$x = r \cdot z$$

$$x = 4 \cdot 3 = 12$$

The value of y

$$y = s \cdot z$$

$$y = 2 \cdot 3 = 6$$

Replace these values into the Diophantine equation

Try again

$$x^5 + y^5 = 1056 \cdot z^5$$

$$12^5 + 6^5 = 1056 \cdot 3^5 = 256608$$

Solution: x = 12, y = 6, z = 3

_____

*) Find the values of x, y, z of the Fermat- Wiles Equation below

$$x^5 + y^5 = 2882 \cdot z^5$$

Unknowns take the whole numbers

Solve

Fermat- Wiles Equation:

$$x^5 + y^5 = 2882 \cdot z^5$$

Applying the popular method

$$\zeta(s) = r^n + s^n = c$$

$$s = \sqrt[n]{c - r^n}$$
$$r = \sqrt[n]{c - s^n}$$
$$\zeta(s) = c \ \& \ \zeta(c) = 0$$
$$x = r \cdot z = \sqrt[n]{c - s^n \cdot z}$$
$$y = s \cdot z = \sqrt[n]{c - r^n \cdot z}$$

$$n \to \infty$$

Find the values of r, s

$$c = 2882$$
$$\zeta(s) = r^5 + s^5 = 2882$$
$$\zeta(s) = 5^5 + (-3)^5 = 2882$$

The values of x, y, z

$$x = r \cdot z$$
$$y = s \cdot z$$

The value of z

Choose any value of z (i.e., 1, 2, 3, 4, 5, 6, 7, 8...)

$$z = 13$$

The value of x

$$x = r \cdot z$$
$$x = 5 \cdot 13 = 65$$

The value of y

$$y = s \cdot z$$
$$y = -3 \cdot 13 = -39$$

Replace these values into the Diophantine equation

Try again

$$x^5 + y^5 = 2882 \cdot z^5$$
$$65^5 + (-39)^5 = 2882 \cdot 13^5 = 1070066426$$

Solution: x = 65, y = -39, z = 13

---

*) Find the values of x, y, z of the Diophantine equation below

$$x^5 + y^5 = z^6$$

Unknowns take the whole numbers

Solve

Diophantine equation:

$$x^5 + y^5 = z^6$$

Rewrite the Diophantine equation to Fermat- Wiles form

$$x^5 + y^5 = z^6$$
$$x^5 + y^5 = z \cdot z^5$$
$$x^5 + y^5 = c \cdot z^5$$

267

Applying the popular method

$$\zeta(s) = r^n + s^n = c$$

$$s = \sqrt[n]{c - r^n}$$
$$r = \sqrt[n]{c - s^n}$$
$$\zeta(s) = c \ \& \ \zeta(c) = 0$$
$$x = r \cdot z = \sqrt[n]{c - s^n \cdot z}$$
$$y = s \cdot z = \sqrt[n]{c - r^n \cdot z}$$

$$n \to \infty$$

Find the values of r, s

We have many values of r and s

Example:

$$\zeta(s) = r^5 + s^5 = c$$
$$\zeta(s)_1 = 3^5 + 2^5 = 275$$
$$\zeta(s)_2 = 4^5 + 3^5 = 1267$$
$$\zeta(s)_3 = 5^5 + 4^5 = 4149$$
$$\zeta(s)_4 = 3^5 + 5^5 = 3368$$
$$\zeta(s)_5 = 5^5 + 2^5 = 3157$$

…

Find the values of x, y, z

By method

$$\zeta(s)_1 = 3^5 + 2^5 = 275$$

The values of x, y, z

$$x = r \cdot z$$
$$y = s \cdot z$$

The value of z

We choose the value of z (z = c ...)

$$z = 275$$

The value of x

$$x = r \cdot z$$
$$x = 3 \cdot 275 = 825$$

The value of y

$$y = s \cdot z$$
$$y = 2 \cdot 275 = 550$$

Replace these values into the equation

Try again

$$x^5 + y^5 = z^6$$
$$825^5 + 550^5 = 275^6 = 432510009765625$$

Solution 1: x = 825, y = 550, z = 275

$$\zeta(s)_2 = 4^5 + 3^5 = 1267$$

The values of x, y, z

$$x = r \cdot z$$
$$y = s \cdot z$$

The value of z

We choose the value of z (z = c ...)

$$z = 1267$$

The value of x

$$x = r \cdot z$$
$$x = 4 \cdot 1267 = 5068$$

The value of y
$$y = s \cdot z$$
$$y = 3 \cdot 1267 = 3801$$

Replace these values into the equation

Try again
$$x^5 + y^5 = z^6$$
$$5068^5 + 3801^5 = 1267^6 = 4136753940852752569$$

Solution 2: x = 5068, y = 3801, z = 1267
$$\zeta(s)_3 = 5^5 + 4^5 = 4149$$

The values of x, y, z
$$x = r \cdot z$$
$$y = s \cdot z$$

The value of z

We choose the value of z (z = c ...)
$$z = 4149$$

The value of x
$$x = r \cdot z$$
$$x = 5 \cdot 4149 = 20745$$

The value of y
$$y = s \cdot z$$
$$y = 4 \cdot 4149 = 16596$$

Replace these values into the equation

Try again

$$x^5 + y^5 = z^6$$

$20745^5 + 16596^5 = 4149^6 = 5101062080473384562601$

Solution 3: x = 20745, y = 16596, z = 4149

$$\zeta(s)_4 = 3^5 + 5^5 = 3368$$

The values of x, y, z

$$x = r \cdot z$$
$$y = s \cdot z$$

The value of z

We choose the value of z (z = c ...)

$$z = 3368$$

The value of x

$$x = r \cdot z$$
$$x = 3 \cdot 3368 = 10104$$

The value of y

$$y = s \cdot z$$
$$y = 5 \cdot 3368 = 16840$$

Replace these values into the equation

Try again

$$x^5 + y^5 = z^6$$

$16840^5 + 10104^5 = 3368^6 = 1459595436886201729024$

Solution 4: x = 16840, y = 10104, z = 3368

$$\zeta(s)_5 = 5^5 + 2^5 = 3157$$

The values of x, y, z

$$x = r \cdot z$$
$$y = s \cdot z$$

The value of z

We choose the value of z (z = c …)

$$z = 3157$$

The value of x

$$x = r \cdot z$$
$$x = 5 \cdot 3157 = 15785$$

The value of y

$$y = s \cdot z$$
$$y = 2 \cdot 3157 = 6314$$

Replace these values into the equation

Try again

$$x^5 + y^5 = z^6$$

$$15785^5 + 6314^5 = 3157^6 = 990028031580072857449$$

Solution 5: x = 15785, y = 6314, z = 3157

---

*) Find the values of x, y, z of the Diophantine equation below

$$x^5 + y^5 = z^7$$

Unknowns take the whole numbers

Applying the popular method

$$\zeta(s) = r^n + s^n = c$$

$$s = \sqrt[n]{c - r^n}$$
$$r = \sqrt[n]{c - s^n}$$
$$\zeta(s) = c \ \& \ \zeta(c) = 0$$
$$x = r \cdot z = \sqrt[n]{c - s^n \cdot z}$$
$$y = s \cdot z = \sqrt[n]{c - r^n \cdot z}$$
$$n \to \infty$$

We have

$120893043130724467605504 1^5 +$

$193428869009159148168806 56^5 =$

$\quad\quad 1152924803144876033^7$

$= 2{,}70773947592945254129014542 06114e{+}126$

Solution:

$\quad\quad x = 1208930431307244676055041$

$\quad\quad y = 19342886900915914816880656$

$\quad\quad z = 1152924803144876033$

…

*) Find the values of x, y, z of the Diophantine equation below

$$x^5 + y^5 = z^8$$

Applying the popular method

$$\zeta(s) = r^n + s^n = c$$

$$s = \sqrt[n]{c - r^n}$$
$$r = \sqrt[n]{c - s^n}$$
$$\zeta(s) = c \ \& \ \zeta(c) = 0$$
$$x = r \cdot z = \sqrt[n]{c - s^n \cdot z}$$
$$y = s \cdot z = \sqrt[n]{c - r^n \cdot z}$$

$$n \to \infty$$

We have

Equation 1

$23796791077194895375000^5 + 8031416988553277189062 5^5$

$= 206832575805625^8$

$= 3,3492805240876472939044250253444e+114$

Solution 1

$$x = 23796791077194895375000$$
$$y = 8031416988553277189062 5$$
$$z = 206832575805625$$

Equation 2

$12379400427441447919408906 25^5 +$

$7922816273562526668421700000 0^5 = 115292150675433062 5^8$

$= 3,1217485968336709112226694169008e+144$

Solution 2

$$x = 12379400427441447919408906 25$$
$$y = 79228162735625266684217000000$$
$$z = 115292150675433062 5$$

…

_____

EXERCISES

*) Find the values of x, y, z of the Fermat- Wiles Equation below

$$x^5 + y^5 = 19932 \cdot z^5$$

Unknowns take the whole numbers

*) Find the values of x, y, z of the Fermat- Wiles Equation below

$$x^5 + y^5 = 24583 \cdot z^5$$

Unknowns take the whole numbers

*) Find the values of x, y, z of the Fermat- Wiles Equation below

$$x^5 + y^5 = 24992 \cdot z^5$$

Unknowns take the whole numbers

*) Find the values of x, y, z of the Fermat- Wiles Equation below

$$x^5 + y^5 = 26281 \cdot z^5$$

Unknowns take the whole numbers

*) Find the values of x, y, z of the Fermat- Wiles Equation below

$$x^5 + y^5 = 29643 \cdot z^5$$

Unknowns take the whole numbers

*) Find the values of x, y, z of the Fermat- Wiles Equation below

$$x^5 + y^5 = 31744 \cdot z^5$$

Unknowns take the whole numbers

*) Find the values of x, y, z of the Fermat- Wiles Equation below

$$x^5 + y^5 = 32525 \cdot z^5$$

Unknowns take the whole numbers

*) Find the values of x, y, z of the Fermat- Wiles Equation below

$$x^5 + y^5 = 32736^6$$

Unknowns take the whole numbers

*) Find the values of x, y, z (whole numbers) of the Fermat- Wiles Equation below

$$x^5 + y^5 = 32767^6$$

*) Find the values of x, y, z of the Fermat- Wiles Equation below

$$x^5 + y^5 = 32769^6$$

Unknowns take the whole numbers

*) Find the values of x, y, z of the Fermat- Wiles Equation below

$$x^5 + y^5 = 32800^6$$

Unknowns take the whole numbers

*) Find the values of x, y, z of the Fermat- Wiles Equation below

$$x^5 + y^5 = z^7$$

Unknowns take the whole numbers

*) Find the values of x, y, z of the Fermat- Wiles Equation below

$$x^5 + y^5 = z^7$$

Unknowns take the whole numbers

*) Find the values of x, y, z (whole numbers) of the Fermat- Wiles Equation below

$$x^5 + y^5 = z^7$$

*) Find the values of x, y, z) of the Fermat- Wiles Equation below

$$x^5 + y^5 = z^8$$

Unknowns take the whole numbers

*) Find the values of x, y, z of the Fermat- Wiles Equation below

$$x^5 + y^5 = z^8$$

Unknowns take the whole numbers

APPLICATION

*) There are many candies in candy box, with three different colors, green, yellow and purple, if the 5th powers of the green, and yellow candies, then sum of both, it's equal to the 6th power of purple candies

Given: 3368 purple candies
How many candies of green and yellow?

Solve

We put

A= green candies
B = yellow candies
C = purple candies

We have

$$F_1(s) = A^5 + B^5 = C^6$$
$$F_1(s) = A^5 + B^5 = 3368^6$$

We rewrite $F_1(s)$ to $F_2(s)$

$$F_2(s) = A^5 + B^5 = C \cdot C^5$$

Back to problem Fermat-Wiles equaion

$$x^n + y^n = c \cdot z^n$$

Applying the popular method with n = 5

$$\zeta(s) = r^n + s^n = c$$

$$s = \sqrt[n]{c - r^n}$$
$$r = \sqrt[n]{c - s^n}$$
$$\zeta(s) = c \ \& \ \zeta(c) = 0$$
$$x = r \cdot z = \sqrt[n]{c - s^n \cdot z}$$
$$y = s \cdot z = \sqrt[n]{c - r^n \cdot z}$$

$$n \to \infty$$

The values of A, B, C

$$\zeta(s) = c \text{ and } \zeta(c) = 0$$

Replace C by c

Find the values of r, s

$$c = 3368$$
$$\zeta(s) = r^5 + s^5 = 3368$$
$$\zeta(s)_1 = 3^5 + 5^5 = 3368$$

The values of A, B

$$\zeta(s) = 3^5 + 5^5 = 3368$$
$$A = r \cdot C$$
$$B = s \cdot C$$

The values of A, B

$$C = 3368 \text{ candies}$$
$$A = r \cdot C = 3 \cdot 3368 = 10104 \text{ candies}$$
$$B = s \cdot C = 5 \cdot 3368 = 16840 \text{ candies}$$

Replace these values into $F_1(s)$

Try again

$$F_1(s) = A^5 + B^5 = C^6$$
$$F_1(s) = 10104^5 + 16840^5 = 3368^6$$
$$= 1459595436886201729024$$

Solution:

A = green candies: 10104

B = yellow candies 16840

C = purple candies 3368

———————————————

EXERCISES

*) There are many candies in candy box, with three different colors, green, yellow and purple, if the 5th powers of the green, and yellow candies, then sum of both, it's equal to the 6th power of purple candies

Given: 49575 purple candies
How many candies of green and yellow?

*) There are many candies in candy box, with three different colors, green, yellow and purple, if the 5th powers of the green, and yellow candies, then sum of both, it's equal to the 6th power of purple candies

Given: 372317 purple candies
How many candies of green and yellow?

*) There are many candies in candy box, with three different colors, green, yellow and purple, if the 5th powers of the

green, and yellow candies, then sum of both, it's equal to the 6th power of purple candies

Given: 760399 purple candies
How many candies of green and yellow?

*) There are many candies in candy box, with three different colors, green, yellow and purple, if the 5th powers of the green, and yellow candies, then sum of both, it's equal to the 6th power of purple candies

Given: 540949 purple candies
How many candies of green and yellow?

*) There are many candies in candy box, with three different colors, green, yellow and purple, if the 5th powers of the green, and yellow candies, then sum of both, it's equal to the 6th power of purple candies

Given: 379069 purple candies
How many candies of green and yellow?

*) There are many candies in candy box, with three different colors, green, yellow and purple, if the 5th powers of the

green, and yellow candies, then sum of both, it's equal to the 6th power of purple candies

Given: 265639 purple candies
How many candies of green and yellow?

*) There are many candies in candy box, with three different colors, green, yellow and purple, if the 5th powers of the green, and yellow candies, then sum of both, it's equal to the 6th power of purple candies

Given: 193819 purple candies
How many candies of green and yellow?

*) There are many candies in candy box, with three different colors, green, yellow and purple, if the 5th powers of the green, and yellow candies, then sum of both, it's equal to the 6th power of purple candies

Given: 159049 purple candies
How many candies of green and yellow?

DIOPHANTINE EQUATION
$A^n + B^n + C^n = D^{n+1}$

*) Find the values of A, B, C, D of the Diophantine equation below

$$A^5 + B^5 + C^5 = D^6$$

Unknowns take the whole numbers

Solve

Diophantine equation:

$$A^5 + B^5 + C^5 = D^6$$

We rewrite the Diophantine equation above to this form

$$A^5 + B^5 + C^5 = D^6$$
$$A^5 + B^5 + C^5 = D \cdot D^5 \text{ or}$$
$$A^5 + B^5 + C^5 = d \cdot D^5$$

Then we use the popular method

$$\zeta(s) = r^n + s^n = c$$

$$s = \sqrt[n]{c - r^n}$$
$$r = \sqrt[n]{c - s^n}$$

285

$$\zeta(s) = c \;\&\; \zeta(c) = 0$$
$$x = r \cdot z = \sqrt[n]{c - s^n \cdot z}$$
$$y = s \cdot z = \sqrt[n]{c - r^n \cdot z}$$
$$n \to \infty$$

Find the values of r, s, t,

We have many values of r, s and t

Example:

$$\zeta(s) = r^5 + s^5 + t^5 = d$$
$$\zeta(s)_1 = 2^5 + 1^5 + 3^5 = 276$$
$$\zeta(s)_2 = 3^5 + 2^5 + 4^5 = 1299$$
$$\zeta(s)_3 = 4^5 + 3^5 + 5^5 = 4392$$
$$\zeta(s)_4 = 1^5 + 2^5 + 6^5 = 7809$$

Back to Diophantine equation

$$A^5 + B^5 + C^5 = d \cdot D^5$$
$$\zeta(s)_1 = 2^5 + 1^5 + 3^5 = 276$$

Similarly

The values of A, B, C

$$A = r \cdot D$$
$$B = s \cdot D$$
$$C = t \cdot D$$

The value of D

We choose the value of D (D = d)

$$D = 276$$

The value of A

$$A = r \cdot D$$
$$A = 2 \cdot 276 = 552$$

The value of B

$$B = s \cdot D$$
$$B = 1 \cdot 276 = 276$$

The value of C

$$C = t \cdot D$$
$$C = 3 \cdot 276 = 828$$

Replace these values into the equation

Try again

$$A^5 + B^5 + C^5 = D^6$$
$$552^5 + 276^5 + 828^5 = 276^6$$
$$= 442032795979776$$

Solution 1: A = 552, B = 276,

$$C = 828, D = 276$$

$$\zeta(s)_2 = 3^5 + 2^5 + 4^5 = 1299$$

Similarly

The values of A, B, C
$$A = r \cdot D$$
$$B = s \cdot D$$
$$C = t \cdot D$$

The value of D
We choose the value of D (D = d)
$$D = 1299$$

The value of A
$$A = r \cdot D$$
$$A = 3 \cdot 1299 = 3897$$
The value of B
$$B = s \cdot D$$
$$B = 2 \cdot 1299 = 2598$$
The value of C
$$C = t \cdot D$$
$$C = 4 \cdot 1299 = 5196$$

Replace these values into the equation
Try again
$$A^5 + B^5 + C^5 = D^6$$
$$3897^5 + 2598^5 + 5196^5 = 1299^6$$
$$= 4804574217585342201$$

Solution 2: A = 3897, B = 2598,

C = 5196, D = 1299

$$\zeta(s)_3 = 4^5 + 3^5 + 5^5 = 4392$$

Similarly

The values of A, B, C

A = r · D

B = s · D

C = t · D

The value of D

We choose the value of D (D = d)

D = 4392

The value of A

A = r · D

A = 4 · 4392 = 17568

The value of B

B = s · D

B = 3 · 4392 = 13176

The value of C

C = t · D

C = 5 · 4392 = 21960

Replace these values into the equation

Try again

$$A^5 + B^5 + C^5 = D^6$$

$$17568^5 + 13176^5 + 21960^5 = 4392^6$$

$$= 7177513014600453586944$$

Solution 3: A = 17568, B = 13176,

C = 21960, D = 4392

$$\zeta(s)_4 = 1^5 + 2^5 + 6^5 = 7809$$

Similarly

The values of A, B, C

A = r · D

B = s · D

C = t · D

The value of D

We choose the value of D (D = d)

D = 7809

The value of A

A = r · D

A = 1 · 7809 = 7809

The value of B

B = s · D

B = 2 · 7809 = 15618

The value of C

$$C = t \cdot D$$
$$C = 6 \cdot 7809 = 46854$$

Replace these values into the equation

Try again

$$A^5 + B^5 + C^5 = D^6$$
$$7809^5 + 15618^5 + 46854^5 = 7809^6$$
$$= 226763179116982492624641$$

Solution 4: A = 7809, B = 15618,

C = 46854, D = 7809

EXERCISES

*) Find the values of A, B, C, of the Diophantine equation below

$$A^5 + B^5 + C^5 = 4392^6$$

Unknowns take the whole numbers

*) Find the values of A, B, C, of the Diophantine equation below

$$A^5 + B^5 + C^5 = 11925^6$$

Unknowns take the whole numbers

*) Find the values of A, B, C, of the Diophantine equation below

$$A^5 + B^5 + C^5 = 11144^6$$

Unknowns take the whole numbers

*) Find the values of A, B, C, of the Diophantine equation below

$$A^5 + B^5 + C^5 = 34035^6$$

Unknowns take the whole numbers

*) Find the values of A, B, C, of the Diophantine equation below

$$A^5 + B^5 + C^5 = 17082^6$$

Unknowns take the whole numbers

*) Find the values of A, B, C, of the Diophantine equation below

$$A^5 + B^5 + C^5 = 1102998412178^7$$

Unknowns take the whole numbers

*) Find the values of A, B, C, of the Diophantine equation below

$$A^5 + B^5 + C^5 = 1102999460753^7$$

Unknowns take the whole numbers

*) Find the values of A, B, C, of the Diophantine equation below

$$A^5 + B^5 + C^5 = 96466943268402^7$$

Unknowns take the whole numbers

*) Find the values of A, B, C, of the Diophantine equation below

$$A^5 + B^5 + C^5 = 3751525871703602^7$$

Unknowns take the whole numbers

*) Find the values of A, B, C, of the Diophantine equation below

$$A^5 + B^5 + C^5 = 31591352717^8$$

Unknowns take the whole numbers

_____

APPLICATION

*) There are 2304 candies in candy box, with four different colors: red, green, yellow and purple

If the cube the red, blue, and yellow candies, then sum all of three, it's equal to multiple 3158 by the cube purple candies

How many candies of each color?

Solve

We put

A= red candy

B = green candy

C = yellow candy

D = purple candy

We have

$$F_1(s) = A + B + C + D = 2304$$

$$F_2(s) = A^5 + B^5 + C^5 = 3158 \cdot D^5$$

Back to Fermat-Wiles equaion

$$x^n + y^n = c \cdot z^n$$

Applying the popular method with n = 5

$$\zeta(s) = r^n + s^n = c$$

$$s = \sqrt[n]{c - r^n}$$
$$r = \sqrt[n]{c - s^n}$$
$$\zeta(s) = c \text{ \& } \zeta(c) = 0$$
$$x = r \cdot z = \sqrt[n]{c - s^n \cdot z}$$
$$y = s \cdot z = \sqrt[n]{c - r^n \cdot z}$$

$$n \to \infty$$

The values of A, B, C, d

$$\zeta(s) = d \text{ and } \zeta(d) = 0$$
$$F_2(s) = A^5 + B^5 + C^5 = d \cdot D^5$$

Find the values of r, s, t

$$d = 3158$$
$$\zeta(s) = r^5 + s^5 + t^5 = d = 3158$$
$$\zeta(s) = 1^5 + 2^5 + 5^5 = 3158$$

The Values of A, B, C, D

$$\zeta(s) = 1^5 + 2^5 + 5^5 = 3158$$
$$A = r \cdot D$$
$$B = s \cdot D$$
$$C = t \cdot D$$

The value of D

We have

$$F_1(s) = A + B + C + D = 2304$$

And

$$r + s + t = 1 + 2 + 5 = 8$$

Then

$$D = \frac{2304}{r + s + t + 1} = \frac{2304}{9} = 256$$

The values of A, B, C

D = 17 candies

A = r · D = 1 · 256 = 256 candies

B = s · D = 2 · 256 = 512 candies

C = t · D = 5 · 256 = 1280 candies

Replace these values into $F_1(s)$ and $F_2(s)$

Try again

$$F_1(s) = A + B + C + D = 2304$$

$$F_1(s) = 1280 + 512 + 256 + 256 = 2304$$

$$F_2(s) = A^5 + B^5 + C^5 = 3158 \cdot D^5$$

$$F_2(s) = 1280^5 + 512^5 + 256^5 = 3158 \cdot 256^5$$

$$= 3472257720516608$$

Solution:

$$D = 256 \text{ candies}$$
$$A = 1280 \text{ candies}$$
$$B = 512 \text{ candies}$$
$$C = 256 \text{ candies}$$

_____

*) There are many candies in candy box, with four different colors red, green, yellow and purple.

If 5th powers of the green, and yellow candies, then sum all of three colors, it's equal to the 6th power of purple candies

Given: 1299 purple candies

How many candies of green and yellow?

Solve

We put

$$A = \text{red candies}$$
$$B = \text{green candies s}$$
$$C = \text{yellow candies}$$
$$D = \text{purple candies}$$

We have

$$F_1(s) = A^5 + B^5 + C^5 = D^6$$
$$F_1(s) = A^5 + B^5 + C^5 = 1299^6$$

We rewrite $F_1(s)$ to $F_2(s)$

$$F_1(s) = A^5 + B^5 + C^5 = D \cdot D^5$$

Back to problem Fermat-Wiles equaion

$$x^n + y^n = c \cdot z^n$$

Applying the popular method with $n = 5$

$$\zeta(s) = r^n + s^n = c$$

$$s = \sqrt[n]{c - r^n}$$
$$r = \sqrt[n]{c - s^n}$$
$$\zeta(s) = c \ \& \ \zeta(c) = 0$$
$$x = r \cdot z = \sqrt[n]{c - s^n} \cdot z$$
$$y = s \cdot z = \sqrt[n]{c - r^n} \cdot z$$

$$n \to \infty$$

The values of A, B, C,D

$$\zeta(s) = c \text{ and } \zeta(c) = 0$$

Replace D by d

Find the values of r, s, t

$$d = 1299$$
$$\zeta(s) = r^5 + s^5 + t^5 = 1299$$
$$\zeta(s)_1 = 2^5 + 3^5 + 4^5 = 1299$$

The values of A, B

$$\zeta(s) = 2^5 + 3^5 + 4^5 = 1299$$
$$A = r \cdot D$$

$$B = s \cdot D$$
$$C = t \cdot D$$

The values of A, B

$$D = 1299 \text{ candies}$$
$$A = r \cdot C = 2 \cdot 1299 = 2598 \text{ candies}$$
$$B = s \cdot C = 3 \cdot 1299 = 3897 \text{ candies}$$
$$C = s \cdot C = 4 \cdot 1299 = 5196 \text{ candies}$$

Replace these values into $F_1(s)$

Try again

$$F_1(s) = A^5 + B^5 + C^5 = D^6$$
$$F_1(s) = 2598^5 + 3897^5 + 5196^5 = 1299^6$$
$$= 4804574217585342201$$

Solution:

A= red candies: 2598

B = green candies: 3897

C = yellow candies: 5196

D = purple candies: 1299

---

*) There are many candies in candy box, with five different colors: red, blue, green, yellow and purple.

If the 5th power of red, blue, green, and yellow candies, then sum all of four colors, it's equal to multiple 4182 by the 5th purple candies

How many candies of each color?

Given: in candy box = 247 candies

Solve

We put

A= red candy

B = Blue candy

C = green candy

D = yellow candy

E = purple candy

We have

$$F_1(s) = A + B + C + D + E = 247$$
$$F_2(s) = A^5 + B^5 + C^5 + D^5 = 4182 \cdot E^5$$

Back to Fermat-Wiles equaion

$$x^n + y^n = c \cdot z^n$$

Applying the popular method with n = 5

$$\zeta(s) = r^n + s^n = c$$

$$s = \sqrt[n]{c - r^n}$$
$$r = \sqrt[n]{c - s^n}$$
$$\zeta(s) = c \ \& \ \zeta(c) = 0$$
$$x = r \cdot z = \sqrt[n]{c - s^n} \cdot z$$

301

$$y = s \cdot z = \sqrt[n]{c - r^n \cdot z}$$

$$n \to \infty$$

The values of A, B, C, D, e

$$\zeta(s) = e \text{ and } \zeta(e) = 0$$

$$F_2(s) = A^5 + B^5 + C^5 + D^5 = e \cdot E^5$$

Find the values of r, s, t, u

$$e = 4182$$

$$\zeta(s) = r^5 + s^5 + t^5 + u^5 = e = 4182$$

$$\zeta(s) = 1^5 + 2^5 + 4^5 + 5^5 = 4182$$

The Values of A, B, C, D

$$\zeta(s) = 1^5 + 2^5 + 4^5 + 5^5 = 4182$$

$$A = r \cdot E$$

$$B = s \cdot E$$

$$C = t \cdot E$$

$$D = u \cdot E$$

The value of E

We have

$$F_1(s) = A + B + C + D + E = 247$$

And

$$r + s + t + u = 1 + 2 + 4 + 5 = 12$$

Then

$$D = \frac{247}{r + s + t + 1} = \frac{247}{13} = 19$$

The values of A, B, C, D

$$E = 19 \text{ candies}$$
$$A = r \cdot E = 1 \cdot 19 = 19 \text{ candies}$$
$$B = s \cdot E = 2 \cdot 19 = 38 \text{ candies}$$
$$C = t \cdot E = 4 \cdot 19 = 76 \text{ candies}$$
$$D = u \cdot E = 5 \cdot 19 = 95 \text{ candies}$$

Replace these values into $F_1(s)$ and $F_2(s)$

Try again

$$F_1(s) = A + B + C + D + E = 247$$
$$F_1(s) = 19 + 38 + 76 + 95 + 19 = 247$$

$$F_2(s) = A^5 + B^5 + C^5 + D^5 = 4182 \cdot E^5$$
$$F_2(s) = 19^5 + 38^5 + 76^5 + 95^5 = 4182 \cdot 19^5$$
$$= 10355046018$$

Solution:

$$A = 19 \text{ candies}$$
$$B = 38 \text{ candies}$$
$$C = 76 \text{ candies}$$
$$D = 95 \text{ candies}$$
$$E = 19 \text{ candies}$$

---

*) There are many candies in candy box, with five different colors: red, blue, green, yellow and purple.

If the 5th power the red, blue, green, and yellow candies, then sum all of four colors, it's equal to multiple 12168 by the 5th power purple candies

How many candies of each color?

Given: in candy box = 437 candies

Solve

We put

A= red candy

B = Blue candy

C = green candy

D = yellow candy

E = purple candy

We have

$$F_1(s) = A + B + C + D + E = 437$$
$$F_2(s) = A^5 + B^5 + C^5 + D^5 = 12168 \cdot E^5$$

Back to Fermat-Wiles equaion

$$x^n + y^n = c \cdot z^n$$

Applying the popular method with n = 5

$$\zeta(s) = r^n + s^n = c$$

$$s = \sqrt[n]{c - r^n}$$
$$r = \sqrt[n]{c - s^n}$$
$$\zeta(s) = c \ \& \ \zeta(c) = 0$$

$$x = r \cdot z = \sqrt[n]{c - s^n \cdot z}$$
$$y = s \cdot z = \sqrt[n]{c - r^n \cdot z}$$

$$n \to \infty$$

The values of A, B, C, D, e

$$\zeta(s) = e \text{ and } \zeta(e) = 0$$
$$F_2(s) = A^5 + B^5 + C^5 + D^5 = e \cdot E^5$$

Find the values of r, s, t, u

$$e = 12168$$
$$\zeta(s) = r^5 + s^5 + t^5 + u^5 = e = 12168$$
$$\zeta(s) = 3^5 + 4^5 + 5^5 + 6^5 = 12168$$

The Values of A, B, C, D

$$\zeta(s) = 3^5 + 4^5 + 5^5 + 6^5 = 12168$$
$$A = r \cdot E$$
$$B = s \cdot E$$
$$C = t \cdot E$$
$$D = u \cdot E$$

The value of E

We have

$$F_1(s) = A + B + C + D + E = 437$$

And

$$r + s + t + u = 3 + 4 + 5 + 6 = 18$$

Then

$$D = \frac{437}{r + s + t + 1} = \frac{437}{19} = 23$$

305

The values of A, B, C, D

$E = 23$ candies

$A = r \cdot E = 3 \cdot 23 = 69$ candies

$B = s \cdot E = 4 \cdot 23 = 92$ candies

$C = t \cdot E = 5 \cdot 23 = 115$ candies

$D = u \cdot E = 6 \cdot 23 = 138$ candies

Replace these values into $F_1(s)$ and $F_2(s)$

Try again

$F_1(s) = A + B + C + D + E = 437$

$F_1(s) = 69 + 92 + 115 + 138 + 23 = 437$

$F_2(s) = A^5 + B^5 + C^5 + D^5 = 12168 \cdot E^5$

$F_2(s) = 69^5 + 92^5 + 115^5 + 138^5 = 12168 \cdot 23^5$

$= 78317421624$

Solution:

$A = 69$ candies

$B = 92$ candies

$C = 115$ candies

$D = 138$ candies

$E = 23$ candies

---

*) There are many candies in candy box, with five different colors: red, blue, green, yellow and purple.

If the 5th powers red, green, blue and yellow candies, then sum all of four colors, it's equal to the 6th power of purple candies

Given: 3401 purple candies
How many candies of each color?

Solve

We put

A= red candies

B = green candies

C = Blue candies

D = yellow candies

E = purple candies

We have

$$F_1(s) = A^5 + B^5 + C^5 + D^5 = E^6$$
$$F_1(s) = A^5 + B^5 + C^5 + D^5 = 3401^6$$

We rewrite $F_1(s)$ to $F_2(s)$
$$F_1(s) = A^5 + B^5 + C^5 + D^5 = E \cdot E^5$$

Back to problem Fermat-Wiles equaion
$$x^n + y^n = c \cdot z^n$$

Applying the popular method, n = 5

$$\zeta(s) = r^n + s^n = c$$

$$s = \sqrt[n]{c - r^n}$$
$$r = \sqrt[n]{c - s^n}$$
$$\zeta(s) = c \ \& \ \zeta(c) = 0$$
$$x = r \cdot z = \sqrt[n]{c - s^n \cdot z}$$
$$y = s \cdot z = \sqrt[n]{c - r^n \cdot z}$$

$$n \to \infty$$

The values of A, B, C,D

$$\zeta(s) = c \text{ and } \zeta(c) = 0$$

Replace E by e

Find the values of r, s, t, u

$$e = 3401$$
$$\zeta(s) = r^5 + s^5 + t^5 + u^5 = 3401$$
$$\zeta(s) = 1^5 + 2^5 + 3^5 + 5^5 = 3401$$

The values of A, B, C, D

$$\zeta(s) = 1^5 + 2^5 + 3^5 + 5^5 = 3401$$
$$A = r \cdot E$$
$$B = s \cdot E$$
$$C = t \cdot E$$
$$D = u \cdot E$$

The values of A, B

E = 1299 candies

A = r · E = 1 · 3401 = 3401 candies

B = s · E = 2 · 3401 = 6802 candies

C = t · E = 3 · 3401 = 10203 candies

D = u · E = 5 · 3401 = 17005 candies

Replace these values into $F_1(s)$

Try again

$$F_1(s) = A^5 + B^5 + C^5 + D^5 = E^6$$

$$F_1(s) = 3401^5 + 6802^5 + 10203^5 + 17005^5 = 3401^6$$

$$= 1547532546730253420401$$

Solution:

A= red candies: 3401

B = green candies: 6802

C = blue candies: 10203

D = yellow candies: 17005

E = purple candies: 3401

_____

EXERCISES

*) There are many candies in candy box, with four different colors red, green, yellow and purple.

If the 5th powers of the red, green, and yellow candies, then sum all of three, it's equal to the 6th power of purple candies

Given: 11925 purple candies
How many candies of each color?

*) There are many candies in candy box, with four different colors red, green, yellow and purple.

If the 5th powers of the red, green, and yellow candies, then sum all of three, it's equal to the 6th power of purple candies

Given: 27708 purple candies
How many candies of of each color?

*) There are many candies in candy box, with four different colors red, green, yellow and purple.

If the 5th powers of the red, green, and yellow candies, then sum all of three, it's equal to the 6th power of purple candies

Given: 24615 purple candies
How many candies of of each color?

*) There are many candies in candy box, with four different colors red, green, yellow and purple.
If the 5th powers of the red, green, and yellow candies, then sum all of three, it's equal to the 6th power of purple candies

Given: 49576 purple candies
How many candies of of each color?

*) There are many candies in candy box, with four different colors red, green, yellow and purple.
If the 5th powers of the red, green, and yellow candies, then sum all of three, it's equal to the 6th power of purple candies

Given: 4424 purple candies
How many candies of of each color?

*) There are many candies in candy box, with four different colors red, green, yellow and purple.

If the 5th powers of the red, green, and yellow candies, then sum all of three, it's equal to the 6th power of purple candies

Given: 4393 purple candies
How many candies of of each color?

*) There are many candies in candy box, with four different colors red, green, yellow and purple.
If the 5th powers of the red, green, and yellow candies, then sum all of three, it's equal to the 6th power of purple candies

Given: 11926 purple candies
How many candies of of each color?

*) There are many candies in candy box, with four different colors red, green, yellow and purple.
If the 5th powers of the red, green, and yellow candies, then sum all of three, it's equal to the 6th power of purple candies

Given: 20957 purple candies
How many candies of of each color?

FERMAT-WILES EQUATION
$x^n + y^n = c\ z^n\ n = 6$

$$x^6 + y^6 = c{\cdot}z^6$$

On the internet

We don't see the table of values of c, with n = 6

Similarly above, I find the value of c by my popular method

My table of values of c with n = 6

2, 65, 128, 730, 793, 1458, 4097, 4160, 4825, 8192, 15626,
15689, 16354, 19721, 31250, 46657, 46720, 50752, 62281,
93312, 117650, 117713, 118378, 121745, 133274, 164305,
235298, 262145, 262208, 262873, 266240, 277769, 308800,
379793, 524288, 531442, 531505, 532170, 535537, 547066,
578097, 649090, 793585, 1062882, 1000001, 1000064,
1000729, 1004096, 1015625, 1046656, 1117649, 1262144,
1531441, 1771562, 1771625, 1772290, 1775657, 1787186,
1818217, 1889210, 2000000, 2033705, 2303002, 2771561,
2985985, 2986048, 2986713, 2990080, 3001609, 3032640,
3103633, 3248128, 3517425. 3543122, 3985984, 4826810,
4826873, 4827538, 4830905, 4842434, 4873465, 4944458,
5088953, 5358250, 5826809, 5971968, 6598370, 7529537,

313

7529600, 7530265, 7533632, 7545161, 7576192, 7647185, 7791680, 7812793, 8060977, 8529536, …

Applying the popular method below

$$\zeta(s) = r^n + s^n = c$$

$$s = \sqrt[n]{c - r^n}$$
$$r = \sqrt[n]{c - s^n}$$
$$\zeta(s) = c \ \& \ \zeta(c) = 0$$
$$x = r \cdot z = \sqrt[n]{c - s^n \cdot z}$$
$$y = s \cdot z = \sqrt[n]{c - r^n \cdot z}$$

$$n \to \infty$$

The values of c with n = 6

$r^6 + s^6 = c$	$4^6 + (-1)^6 = 4097$
$1^6 + 1^6 = 2$	$4^6 + 1^6 = 4097$
$(-)1^6 + 2^6 = 65$	$4^6 + 2^6 = 4160$
$1^6 + 2^6 = 65$	$4^6 + 3^6 = 4825$
$2^6 + 2^6 = 128$	$4^6 + 4^6 = 8192$
$(-2)^6 + 3^6 = 793$	$5^6 + (-4)^6 = 19721$
$(-1)^6 + 3^6 = 730$	$5^6 + (-3)^6 = 16354$
$1^6 + 3^6 = 730$	$5^6 + (-2)^6 = 15689$
$2^6 + 3^6 = 793$	$5^6 + (-1)^6 = 15626$
$3^6 + 3^6 = 1458$	$5^6 + 1^6 = 15626$
$4^6 + (-3)^6 = 4825$	$5^6 + 2^6 = 15689$
$4^6 + (-2)^6 = 4160$	$5^6 + 3^6 = 16354$

314

$5^6 + 4^6 = 19721$

$6^6 + (-5)^6 = 62281$

$5^6 + 5^6 = 31250$

$6^6 + (-4)^6 = 50752$

$6^6 + (-3)^6 = 47385$

$6^6 + (-2)^6 = 46720$

$6^6 + (-1)^6 = 46657$

...

$6^6 + 1^6 = 46657$

$6^6 + 2^6 = 46720$

$6^6 + 3^6 = 47385$

$6^6 + 4^6 = 50752$

$6^6 + 5^6 = 62281$

APPLICATION

*) Find the values of x, y, z (whole numbers) of the Fermat-Wiles Equation below

$$x^6 + y^6 = 4160 \cdot z^6$$

Solve

Fermat- Wiles Equation:

$$x^6 + y^6 = 4160 \cdot z^6$$

Applying the popular method

$$\zeta(s) = r^n + s^n = c$$

$$s = \sqrt[n]{c - r^n}$$
$$r = \sqrt[n]{c - s^n}$$
$$\zeta(s) = c \ \& \ \zeta(c) = 0$$
$$x = r \cdot z = \sqrt[n]{c - s^n \cdot z}$$
$$y = s \cdot z = \sqrt[n]{c - r^n \cdot z}$$

$$n \to \infty$$

Find the values of r, s

$$c = 4160$$
$$\zeta(s) = r^6 + s^6 = 4160$$
$$\zeta(s)_1 = 2^6 + 4^6 = 4160$$
$$\zeta(s)_2 = (-2)^6 + 4^6 = 4160$$
$$\zeta(s)_1 = 2^6 + 4^6 = 4160$$

The values of x, y, z

$$x = r \cdot z$$
$$y = s \cdot z$$

The value of z

Choose any value of z (i.e., 1, 2, 3, 4, 5, 6, 7,...)

$$z = 6$$

The value of x

$$x = r \cdot z$$
$$x = 2 \cdot 6 = 12$$

The value of y

$$y = s \cdot z$$
$$y = 4 \cdot 6 = 24$$

Replace these values into the equation

Try again

$$x^6 + y^6 = 4160 \cdot z^6$$
$$12^6 + 24^6 = 4160 \cdot 6^6 = 194088960$$

Solution1: x = 12, y = 24, z = 6

$$\zeta(s)_2 = (-2)^6 + 4^6 = 4160$$

The values of x, y, z

$$x = r \cdot z$$
$$y = s \cdot z$$

The value of z

Choose any value of z (i.e., 1, 2, 3, 4, 5, 6, 7,...)

$$z = 6$$

The value of x

$$x = r \cdot z$$
$$x = -2 \cdot 6 = -12$$

The value of y

$$y = s \cdot z$$
$$y = 4 \cdot 6 = 24$$

Replace these values into the equation

Try again

$$x^6 + y^6 = 4160 \cdot z^6$$
$$(-12)^6 + 24^6 = 4160 \cdot 6^6 = 194088960$$

Solution2: x = -12, y = 24, z = 6

_____

*) Find the values of x, y, z (whole numbers) of the Fermat-Wiles Equation below

$$x^6 + y^6 = 50752 \cdot z^6$$

Solve

Fermat- Wiles Equation:

$$x^6 + y^6 = 50752 \cdot z^6$$

Applying the popular method

$$\zeta(s) = r^n + s^n = c$$
$$s = \sqrt[n]{c - r^n}$$
$$r = \sqrt[n]{c - s^n}$$
$$\zeta(s) = c \ \& \ \zeta(c) = 0$$
$$x = r \cdot z = \sqrt[n]{c - s^n} \cdot z$$
$$y = s \cdot z = \sqrt[n]{c - r^n} \cdot z$$

$$n \to \infty$$

Find the values of r, s

$$c = 50752$$
$$\zeta(s) = r^6 + s^6 = 50752$$
$$\zeta(s)_1 = 6^6 + 4^6 = 50752$$
$$\zeta(s)_2 = 6^6 + (-4)^6 = 50752$$

$$\zeta(s)_1 = 6^6 + 4^6 = 50752$$

The values of x, y, z

$$x = r \cdot z$$
$$y = s \cdot z$$

The value of z

Choose any value of z (i.e., 1, 2, 3, 4, 5, 6, 7,...)

$$z = 7$$

The value of x

$$x = r \cdot z$$
$$x = 6 \cdot 7 = 42$$

The value of y

$$y = s \cdot z$$
$$y = 4 \cdot 7 = 28$$

Replace these values into the equation

Try again

$$x^6 + y^6 = 50752 \cdot z^6$$
$$42^6 + 28^6 = 50752 \cdot 7^6 = 5970922048$$

Solution1: x = 42, y = 28, z = 7

$$\zeta(s)_2 = 6^6 + (-4)^6 = 50752$$

The values of x, y, z

$$x = r \cdot z$$
$$y = s \cdot z$$

The value of z

Choose any value of z (i.e., 1, 2, 3, 4, 5, 6, 7,...)

$$z = 7$$

The value of x

$$x = r \cdot z$$
$$x = 6 \cdot 7 = 42$$

The value of y

$$y = s \cdot z$$
$$y = -4 \cdot 6 = -24$$

Replace these values into the equation

Try again

$$x^6 + y^6 = 50752 \cdot z^6$$
$$42^6 + (-24)^6 = 50752 \cdot 6^6 = 194088960$$

Solution2: x = 42, y = -24, z = 7

---

*) Find the values of x, y, z of the Diophantine equation below

$$x^6 + y^6 = z^7$$

unknowns take the whole numbers

Solve

Diophantine equation:

$$x^6 + y^6 = z^7$$

Rewrite the Diophantine equation to Fermat- Wiles form

$$x^6 + y^6 = z^7$$
$$x^6 + y^6 = z \cdot z^6$$
$$x^6 + y^6 = c \cdot z^6$$

Applying the popular method

$$\zeta(s) = r^n + s^n = c$$

$$s = \sqrt[n]{c - r^n}$$
$$r = \sqrt[n]{c - s^n}$$

$$\zeta(s)\text{=c} \ \& \ \zeta(c) = 0$$
$$\text{x=r} \cdot \text{z=}^{n}\sqrt{c - s^{n} \cdot z}$$
$$\text{y=s} \cdot \text{z=}^{n}\sqrt{c - r^{n} \cdot z}$$

$$n \rightarrow \infty$$

Find the values of r, s

We have many values of r and s

Example:

$$\zeta(s) = r^6 + s^6 = c$$
$$\zeta(s)_1 = 1^6 + 2^6 = 65$$
$$\zeta(s)_2 = 2^6 + 3^6 = 793$$
$$\zeta(s)_3 = 2^6 + 4^6 = 4160$$
$$\zeta(s)_4 = 4^6 + 3^6 = 4825$$
$$\zeta(s)_5 = 4^6 + 4^6 = 8192$$

…

So we have countless values of x, y, z

By method

$$\zeta(s)_1 = 1^6 + 2^6 = 65$$

The values of x, y, z

$$x = r \cdot z$$
$$y = s \cdot z$$

The value of z

We choose the value of z (z = c …)

$$z = 65$$

The value of x

$$x = r \cdot z$$
$$x = 1 \cdot 65 = 65$$

The value of y

$$y = s \cdot z$$
$$y = 2 \cdot 65 = 130$$

Replace these values into the equation

Try again

$$x^6 + y^6 = z^7$$
$$65^6 + 130^6 = 65^7 = 4902227890625$$

Solution1: x = 65, y = 130, z = 65

$$\zeta(s)_2 = 2^6 + 3^6 = 793$$

Similarly

The values of x, y, z

$$x = r \cdot z$$
$$y = s \cdot z$$

The value of z

We choose the value of z (z = c …)

$$z = 793$$

The value of x

$$x = r \cdot z$$
$$x = 2 \cdot 793 = 1586$$

The value of y

$$y = s \cdot z$$
$$y = 3 \cdot 793 = 2379$$

Replace these values into the equation

Try again

$$x^6 + y^6 = z^7$$

$1586^6 + 2379^6 = 793^7 = 197202452272691930857$

Solution 2: x = 1586, y = 2379, z = 793

$$\zeta(s)_3 = 2^6 + 4^6 = 4160$$

Similarly

The values of x, y, z

$$x = r \cdot z$$
$$y = s \cdot z$$

The value of z

We choose the value of z (z = c …)

$$z = 4160$$

The value of x

$$x = r \cdot z$$
$$x = 2 \cdot 4160 = 8320$$

The value of y

$$y = s \cdot z$$
$$y = 4 \cdot 4160 = 16640$$

Replace these values into the equation

Try again

$$x^6 + y^6 = z^7$$

$8320^6 + 16640^6 = 4160^7 = 2156022627100000002560000000$

Solution 3: x = 8320, y = 16640, z = 4160

$$\zeta(s)_4 = 4^6 + 3^6 = 4825$$

Similarly

The values of x, y, z

$$x = r \cdot z$$
$$y = s \cdot z$$

The value of z

We choose the value of z (z = c ...)

$$z = 4825$$

The value of x

$$x = r \cdot z$$
$$x = 4 \cdot 4825 = 19300$$

The value of y

$$y = s \cdot z$$
$$y = 3 \cdot 4825 = 14475$$

Replace these values into the equation

Try again

$$x^6 + y^6 = z^7$$

$$19300^6 + 14475^6 = 4825^7 = 608809223999332092228515625$$

Solution 4: x = 19300, y = 114475, z = 4825

$$\zeta(s)_5 = 4^6 + 4^6 = 8192$$

Similarly

The values of x, y, z

$$x = r \cdot z$$
$$y = s \cdot z$$

The value of z

We choose the value of z (z = c ...)

$$z = 8192$$

The value of x

$$x = r \cdot z$$
$$x = 4 \cdot 8192 = 32768$$

The value of y

$$y = s \cdot z$$
$$y = 4 \cdot 8192 = 32768$$

Replace these values into the equation

Try again

$$x^6 + y^6 = z^7$$

$$32768^6 + 32768^6 = 8192^7 = 2475880078570760549798248448$$

Solution 4: x = 32768, y = 32768, z = 4825

EXERCISES

*) Find the values of x, y, z (whole numbers) of the Fermat-Wiles Equation below

$$x^6 + y^6 = 3543122 \cdot z^6$$

*) Find the values of x, y, z (whole numbers) of the Fermat-Wiles Equation below

$$x^6 + y^6 = 4830905 \cdot z^6$$

*) Find the values of x, y, z (whole numbers) of the Fermat-Wiles Equation below

$$x^6 + y^6 = 3985984 \cdot z^6$$

*) Find the values of x, y, z (whole numbers) of the Fermat-Wiles Equation below

$$x^6 + y^6 = 4826810 \cdot z^6$$

*) Find the values of x, y, z (whole numbers) of the Fermat-Wiles Equation below

$$x^6 + y^6 = 4826873 \cdot z^6$$

*) Find the values of x, y, z (whole numbers) of the Fermat-Wiles Equation below

$$x^6 + y^6 = 4827538{\cdot}z^6$$

*) Find the values of x, y, z (whole numbers) of the Fermat-Wiles Equation below

$$x^6 + y^6 = 4842434^7$$

*) Find the values of x, y, z (whole numbers) of the Fermat-Wiles Equation below

$$x^6 + y^6 = 5826809^7$$

*) Find the values of x, y, z (whole numbers) of the Fermat-Wiles Equation below

$$x^6 + y^6 = 5358250^7$$

*) Find the values of x, y, z (whole numbers) of the Fermat-Wiles Equation below

$$x^6 + y^6 = 5088953^7$$

*) Find the values of x, y, z (whole numbers) of the Fermat-Wiles Equation below

$$x^6 + y^6 = 4944458^7$$

*) Find the values of x, y, z (whole numbers) of the Fermat-Wiles Equation below

$$x^6 + y^6 = 4873465^7$$

*) Find the values of x, y, z (whole numbers) of the Fermat-Wiles Equation below

$$x^6 + y^6 = 7529537^7$$

*) Find the values of x, y, z (whole numbers) of the Fermat-Wiles Equation below

$$x^6 + y^6 = 6598370^7$$

DIOPHANTINE EQUATION
$A^n + B^n + C^n = D^{n+1}$

*) Find the values of A, B, C, D of the Diophantine equation below

$$A^6 + B^6 + C^6 = D^7$$

Unknowns take the whole numbers

Solve

Diophantine equation:

$$A^6 + B^6 + C^6 = D^7$$

We rewrite the Diophantine equation above to this form

$$A^6 + B^6 + C^6 = D^7$$
$$A^6 + B^6 + C^6 = D \cdot D^6 \text{ or}$$
$$A^6 + B^6 + C^6 = d \cdot D^6$$

Then we use the popular method

$$\zeta(s) = r^n + s^n = c$$

$$s = \sqrt[n]{c - r^n}$$

$$r = \sqrt[n]{c - s^n}$$
$$\zeta(s) = c \; \& \; \zeta(c) = 0$$
$$x = r \cdot z = \sqrt[n]{c - s^n} \cdot z$$
$$y = s \cdot z = \sqrt[n]{c - r^n} \cdot z$$
$$n \to \infty$$

Find the values of r, s, t,

We have many values of r, s and t

Example:

$$\zeta(s) = r^6 + s^6 + t^6 = d$$
$$\zeta(s)_1 = 1^6 + 2^6 + 5^6 = 15690$$
$$\zeta(s)_2 = 2^6 + 1^6 + 3^6 = 794$$
$$\zeta(s)_3 = 2^6 + 3^6 + 4^6 = 4889$$
$$\zeta(s)_4 = 1^6 + 3^6 + 5^6 = 16355$$

Back to Diophantine equation

$$A^6 + B^6 + C^6 = d \cdot D^6$$
$$\zeta(s)_1 = 1^6 + 2^6 + 5^6 = 15690$$

Similarly

The values of A, B, C

$$A = r \cdot D$$
$$B = s \cdot D$$
$$C = t \cdot D$$

331

The value of D

We choose the value of D (D = d)

$$D = 15690$$

The value of A

$$A = r \cdot D$$
$$A = 1 \cdot 15690 = 15690$$

The value of B

$$B = s \cdot D$$
$$B = 2 \cdot 15690 = 31380$$

The value of C

$$C = t \cdot D$$
$$C = 5 \cdot 15690 = 78450$$

Replace these values into the equation

Try again

$$A^6 + B^6 + C^6 = D^7$$
$$15690^6 + 31380^6 + 78450^6 = 15690^7$$
$$= 2340780037692393085308908900000000$$

Solution 1: A = 15690, B = 31380,

$$C = 78450, D = 15690$$

$$\zeta(s)_2 = 2^6 + 1^6 + 3^6 = 794$$

Similarly

The values of A, B, C

$$A = r \cdot D$$
$$B = s \cdot D$$
$$C = t \cdot D$$

The value of D

We choose the value of D (D = d)

$$D = 794$$

The value of A

$$A = r \cdot D$$
$$A = 2 \cdot 794 = 1588$$

The value of B

$$B = s \cdot D$$
$$B = 1 \cdot 794 = 794$$

The value of C

$$C = t \cdot D$$
$$C = 3 \cdot 794 = 2382$$

Replace these values into the equation

Try again

$$A^6 + B^6 + C^6 = D^7$$
$$1588^6 + 794^6 + 2382^6 = 794^7$$
$$= 198949804624071553664$$

Solution 2: A = 1588, B = 794,

C = 2382, D = 794

$$\zeta(s)_3 = 2^6 + 3^6 + 4^6 = 4889$$

Similarly

The values of A, B, C

$$A = r \cdot D$$
$$B = s \cdot D$$
$$C = t \cdot D$$

The value of D

We choose the value of D (D = d)

$$D = 4889$$

The value of A

$$A = r \cdot D$$
$$A = 2 \cdot 4889 = 9778$$

The value of B

$$B = s \cdot D$$
$$B = 3 \cdot 4889 = 14667$$

The value of C

$$C = t \cdot D$$
$$C = 4 \cdot 4889 = 19556$$

Replace these values into the equation

Try again

$$A^6 + B^6 + C^6 = D^7$$
$$9778^6 + 14667^6 + 19556^6 = 4889^7$$
$$= 6676367907138095403534 5129$$

Solution 3: A = 9778, B = 14667,

$$C = 19556, D = 4889$$

$$\zeta(s)_4 = 1^6 + 3^6 + 5^6 = 16355$$

Similarly

The values of A, B, C

$$A = r \cdot D$$
$$B = s \cdot D$$
$$C = t \cdot D$$

The value of D

We choose the value of D (D = d)

$$D = 16355$$

The value of A

$$A = r \cdot D$$

$$A = 1 \cdot 16355 = 16355$$

The value of B

$$B = s \cdot D$$

$$B = 3 \cdot 16355 = 49065$$

The value of C

$$C = t \cdot D$$

$$C = 5 \cdot 16355 = 81775$$

Replace these values into the equation

Try again

$$A^6 + B^6 + C^6 = D^7$$

$$16355^6 + 49065^6 + 81775^6 = 16355^7$$

$$= 3130068480228767499241 24296875$$

Solution 4: A = 16355, B = 49065,

C = 81775, D = 16355

DIOPHANTINE EQUATION
$A^n + B^n + C^n + D^n = E^{n+1}$

*) Find the values of A, B, C, D, E of the Diophantine equation below

$$A^6 + B^6 + C^6 + D^6 = E^7$$

Unknowns take the whole numbers

Solve

Diophantine equation:

$$A^6 + B^6 + C^6 + D^6 = E^7$$

We rewrite the Diophantine equation above to this form

$$A^6 + B^6 + C^6 + D^6 = E^7$$
$$A^6 + B^6 + C^6 + D^6 = E \cdot E^6 \text{ or}$$
$$A^6 + B^6 + C^6 + D^6 = e \cdot E^6$$

Then we use the popular method

$$\zeta(s) = r^n + s^n = c$$

$$s = \sqrt[n]{c - r^n}$$
$$r = \sqrt[n]{c - s^n}$$
$$\zeta(s) = c \;\&\; \zeta(c) = 0$$
$$x = r \cdot z = \sqrt[n]{c - s^n \cdot z}$$
$$y = s \cdot z = \sqrt[n]{c - r^n \cdot z}$$

$$n \to \infty$$

Find the values of r, s, t, u

We have many values of r, s, t and u

Example:

$$\zeta(s) = r^6 + s^6 + t^6 + u^6 = e$$
$$\zeta(s)_1 = 1^6 + 2^6 + 3^6 + 4^6 = 4890$$
$$\zeta(s)_2 = 2^6 + 1^6 + 4^6 + 5^6 = 19786$$
$$\zeta(s)_3 = 3^6 + 4^6 + 2^6 + 5^6 = 20514$$
$$\zeta(s)_4 = 4^6 + 5^6 + 1^6 + 6^6 = 66378$$

Back to Diophantine equation

$$A^6 + B^6 + C^6 + D^6 = E^7$$
$$\zeta(s)_1 = 1^6 + 2^6 + 3^6 + 4^6 = 4890$$

Similarly

The values of A, B, C, D

$$A = r \cdot E$$
$$B = s \cdot E$$

337

$$C = t \cdot E$$
$$D = u \cdot E$$

The value of E

We choose the value of E (E = e)

$$E = 4890$$

The value of A

$$A = r \cdot E$$
$$A = 1 \cdot 4890 = 4890$$

The value of B

$$B = s \cdot E$$
$$B = 2 \cdot 4890 = 9780$$

The value of C

$$C = t \cdot E$$
$$C = 3 \cdot 4890 = 14670$$

The value of D

$$D = u \cdot E$$
$$D = 4 \cdot 4890 = 19560$$

Replace these values into the equation

Try again

$$A^6 + B^6 + C^6 + D^6 = E^7$$
$$4890^6 + 9780^6 + 14670^6 + 19560^6 = 4890^7$$
$$= 66859329025382263290000000$$

Solution 1: A = 4890, B = 9780,

C = 14670, D = 19560, E = 4890

$\zeta(s)_2 = 2^6 + 1^6 + 4^6 + 5^6 = 19786$

Similarly

The values of A, B, C, D

A = r · E

B = s · E

C = t · E

D = u · E

The value of E

We choose the value of E (E = e)

E = 19786

The value of A

A = r · E

A = 2 · 19786 = 39572

The value of B

B = s · E

B = 1 · 19786 = 19786

The value of C

C = t · E

C = 4 · 19786 = 79144

The value of D

$$D = u \cdot E$$
$$D = 5 \cdot 19786 = 98930$$

Replace these values into the equation

Try again

$$A^6 + B^6 + C^6 + D^6 = E^7$$

$$39572^6 + 19786^6 + 79144^6 + 98930^6 = 19786^7$$
$$= 11871511927535794178828068116096$$

Solution 2: A = 39572, B = 19786,
C = 79144, D = 98930, E = 19786

$$\zeta(s)_3 = 3^6 + 4^6 + 2^6 + 5^6 = 20514$$

Similarly

The values of A, B, C, D

$$A = r \cdot E$$
$$B = s \cdot E$$
$$C = t \cdot E$$
$$D = u \cdot E$$

The value of E

We chose the value of E (E = e)

$$E = 20514$$

The value of A

$$A = r \cdot E$$
$$A = 3 \cdot 20514 = 61542$$

The value of B

$$B = s \cdot E$$
$$B = 4 \cdot 20514 = 82056$$

The value of C

$$C = t \cdot E$$
$$C = 2 \cdot 20514 = 41028$$

The value of D

$$D = u \cdot E$$
$$D = 5 \cdot 20514 = 102570$$

Replace these values into the equation
Try again

$$A^6 + B^6 + C^6 + D^6 = E^7$$

$$61542^6 + 82056^6 + 41028^6 + 102570^6 = 20514^7$$
$$= 1528806280791416077481849829504$$

Solution 3: A = 61542, B = 82056,
C = 41028, D = 102570, E = 20514

$$\zeta(s)_4 = 4^6 + 5^6 + 1^6 + 6^6 = 66378$$

Similarly

The values of A, B, C, D

$$A = r \cdot E$$
$$B = s \cdot E$$
$$C = t \cdot E$$
$$D = u \cdot E$$

The value of E

We chose the value of E (E = e)

$$E = 66378$$

The value of A

$$A = r \cdot E$$
$$A = 4 \cdot 66378 = 265512$$

The value of B

$$B = s \cdot E$$
$$B = 5 \cdot 66378 = 331890$$

The value of C

$$C = t \cdot E$$
$$C = 1 \cdot 66378 = 66378$$

The value of D

$$D = u \cdot E$$
$$D = 6 \cdot 66378 = 398268$$

Replace these values into the equation

Try again

$$A^6 + B^6 + C^6 + D^6 = E^7$$

$$265512^6 + 331890^6 + 66378^6 + 398268^6 = 66378^7$$

$$= 5,6776568319738444021437225279013e + 33$$

Solution 3: A = 265512, B = 331890,

C = 66378, D = 398268, E = 66378

-------------//////////-----------

Printed in the United States
by Baker & Taylor Publisher Services

Printed in the United States
By Bookmasters